NORSE DIVINATION

About the Author

Gypsey Elaine Teague is a Heathen Gyðja and an Elder in the Georgian Wiccan Tradition. She is the author of *Steampunk Magic: Working Magic Aboard the Airship* and *The Witch's Guide to Wands: A Complete Botanical, Magical, and Elemental Guide to Making, Choosing, and Using the Right Wand*, both published by Red Wheel/Weiser, nineteen novels, and three edited collections on gender. She is the owner of Goðan Daginn, an agro-educational Icelandic farm where she teaches wood, leather, fiber, and metal crafts as the Icelanders practiced them.

Gypsey holds graduate degrees in business administration, landscape architecture, regional and city planning, library and information sciences, and mental health education. She is a second-degree black belt in Kodokan Judo, a Junior Olympic archery coach, and holds the rank of captain in the United States Army Reserve. Gypsey recently retired from Clemson University, where she was an adjunct professor in the Science and Technology Department and a tenured faculty of the College of Libraries as the anthropology and sociology librarian.

At home she lives with her wife, many cats, chickens, and Æsir Svartal Baldrsson, known around the farm as Asa: her half-border collie, half-Icelandic sheepdog.

She may be reached through her website at www.gypseyteague.com.

NORSE DIVINATION

ILLUMINATING YOUR PATH WITH THE WISDOM OF THE GODS

GYPSEY ELAINE TEAGUE

Llewellyn Publications
Woodbury, Minnesota

FIRST EDITION
First Printing, 2021

Book design by Samantha Peterson
Cover design by Shannon McKuhen
Interior art by Llewellyn Art Department
Photo on page 197 by Heather Greene

Llewellyn Publications is a registered trademark of Llewellyn Worldwide Ltd.

Library of Congress Cataloging-in-Publication Data
Names: Teague, Gypsey, author.
Title: Norse divination: illuminating your path with the wisdom of the
    gods / Gypsey Teague.
Description: First edition. | Woodbury, MN : Llewellyn Publications, a
    division of Llewellyn Worldwide, Ltd, 2021. | Includes bibliographical
    references and index. | Summary: "Through concise yet detailed analyses
    of these deities and their relationships to each other, you'll gain a
    deep understanding of your past, present, and future.Learn how to use
    the gods' beliefs, customs, loves, and deaths to create your own
    36-piece"—Provided by publisher.
Identifiers: LCCN 2021036816 (print) | LCCN 2021036817 (ebook) | ISBN
    9780738767727 | ISBN 9780738767796 (ebook)
Subjects: LCSH: Mythology, Norse. | Runes—Miscellanea. | Divination. |
    Cosmology, Norse.
Classification: LCC BL860 .T43 2021 (print) | LCC BL860 (ebook) | DDC
    293/.32—dc23
LC record available at https://lccn.loc.gov/2021036816
LC ebook record available at https://lccn.loc.gov/2021036817

Llewellyn Publications
A Division of Llewellyn Worldwide Ltd.
2143 Wooddale Drive
Woodbury, MN 55125-2989
www.llewellyn.com

Printed in the United States of America

Other Books by Gypsey Elaine Teague

Steampunk Magic: Working Magic Aboard the Airship

*The Witch's Guide to Wands: A Complete Botanical,
Magical, and Elemental Guide to Making,
Choosing, and Using the Right Wand*

NOTE 1: Much of the information on the creation of the nine realms comes from the *Völuspá*. A copy of this is found in the *Hauksbók*, held in the Árni Magnússon Institute for Icelandic Studies. I had an opportunity to study this work in 2014 when I visited the institute with other scholars from Scandinavia.

NOTE 2: There are over two hundred names, places, and items that may be foreign to the reader. Everything that I mention in this book is included in the glossary. If you find something that you are having trouble understanding, start there.

CONTENTS

PART 3: ADDITIONAL ENTITIES   199

ACKNOWLEDGMENTS

First, I want to thank my wife, Marla. She is always there supporting me when I write, and this book would never have gotten started without her support. I want to thank my oldest and dearest friend, Delph, and my Viking daughter, Tanna, for proofing the book multiple times for flaws, omissions, and, gods forbid, grammatical errors. Delph has read every book I've written in draft and has never failed me. I want to thank my editor, Heather Greene, who pitched this book to a room of other editors who probably didn't have much of an idea what I was trying to do here or how I could do it. She made sense out of my proposal and this is the outcome.

Finally, I want to thank the Heathen community, past, present, and those to come. We are small but we are not quiet. We have been around for over a thousand years and we will prevail until and after Ragnarök. I hope I have done them all proud.

Part One

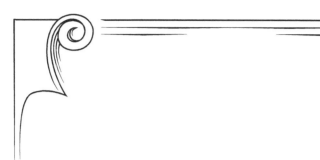

INTRODUCTION

I would love to say that I was born and raised by a Heathen couple who nurtured my interest and desire to learn more about my cultural roots. I would also love to say that I come from a long line of Heathens who can trace my line back to the Northmen of legend. Unfortunately, I cannot say either of these. I was instead raised Catholic. My mother and all my maternal side came from a small town in Quebec Province. My father was nondenominational. My paternal grandmother was Methodist, and my paternal grandfather was Baptist. However, for all these diverse Christian religions, I was exposed early to the Norse culture and history. My family told me I was a little bit Icelandic. I have no proof of that, and thanks to a genetic test I know I am 76 percent Canadian French, with some Irish, Scottish, German, and others thrown in.

I remember having Viking toy soldiers as a very young child. They were the colored plastic ones in preset positions. About three-quarters of an inch high, they were perfect for the long ships I found at Woolworth's in their model department. Then in 1964, *National Geographic* came out with their November issue that discussed the discovery of the settlement at L'Anse aux Meadows in Newfoundland.[1] After that it was more book work and learning who these fascinating people whom I wanted to be related to really were.

By the time I was in high school I began gravitating to the Norse and started studying the culture of the area. I found and started reading the *Thor* comic books put out by Marvel. I know now they weren't accurate, but to a twelve-year-old they were more than what I could ask for. They were the stories of *my* gods, albeit skewed for the reading public of the twentieth century. I learned what little Icelandic I could at home growing up, but promptly forgot it when I had to take German and Latin in high school. I read the sagas and envisioned myself sailing with Leifr Erikson. By my early twenties I was an army officer and learning to be a Gyðja, a leader of the blots, the sacred rituals performed at specific spiritual times of the year. In my thirties I was posted all over the world: twice to Korea, once to Japan, once to Germany, but Iceland was always home to me, even though I had yet to visit.

Birth of the New Divination System

It was at that time that I began learning the runes—those foreign letters on small pieces of stone sold at gift shops or made by friends. I have two sets still from that time. One set I made when I had a ceramic shop in Oklahoma and another set was gifted to me by a member of our troth, our group of Heathens. The set that was a gift is ebony wood made into the pieces with Osage orange wood inlay. These runes were strange and wonderful and a doorway into something that I had no idea about.

First, I studied the Elder Futhark, the early carved letters and symbols of the Germanic people as they migrated north and west toward the snowy climes of Scandinavia, roughly 300 to 600 CE. After that I began going

---

1. Helge Ingstad, "Vinland Ruins Prove Vikings Found the New World," *National Geographic,* National Geographic Society, Washington, D.C. 126, no. 5 (November 1964): 708–734.

through the Younger Futhark and the medieval period of the Vikings and how they simplified and shortened the alphabet for their people.

It is here I should explain what the Futhark is. The word "Futhark" represents the first six letters of the Norse alphabet. The letters look like this: ᚠᚢᚦᚨᚱᚲ. The ᚦ is named "thorn" and is pronounced "th." It is the third letter of the word, and the word then is spelled "Futhark." There are twenty-four letters in the Elder Futhark. Eventually many of them became letters we now recognize, but that was after hundreds of years and many other cultures tinkering with them. During the Norse time these were the only writing there was. Odin hung from the great ash Yggdrasil for nine days and nights to understand the runes and their usage and they represent the magic and the wisdom of the Norse age. These are also the runes that seers study in order to tell the past, the present, and the future.[2] Eventually the Younger Futhark dropped eight symbols and became the sixteen that we see on statues and tablets from Kaupang to the Middle East.

For all the books on rune magic and divination, there was always something missing. To me, the gods were ever present, and they were what actually influenced my life. However, I liked the way the rune stones felt in my hands and how they looked; I just couldn't get them to do what I thought they should. So for twenty years I looked for something similar but different. Eventually I thought of the representative pieces while reading a journal article about kennings. A kenning is a way of describing something using language that is not the name of the item or person. A couple that are used often are "the All Father" or "The Wanderer," meaning Odin.

By my forties I had an inkling of what the pieces of a new system were to look like and what they would represent. I did this by looking at the major players in the Norse pantheon and their most important items that they used as gods. I spent months looking at each piece and thinking what they represented in terms of traits. I had used tarot cards before and thought of the cards and their meanings. When the beginning of the system began to coalesce, it made sense that these pieces interacted similar to the tarot.

When I was ready, I found a large wooden dowel in my garage and cut that into pieces. They looked like discs, but they were enough to get me started.

---

2. Teresa Dröfn Freysdóttir Njarðvík, ed., *Runes: The Icelandic Book of Fuþark*, trans. Philip Roughton (Reykjavik: Icelandic Magic Company, 2018), 6.

I made a working set with names written on pieces of cut dowel in marker. They were ugly but they gave me a set to experiment with. It would be another twenty years before I had enough information to formulate the basis for this book and this divination system.

The Pieces

There are thirty-six primary pieces. Please note these pieces are not rune stones. I use runic symbols to differentiate the pieces, but they are just ways to tell the difference between them. Each piece represents either a person or a thing. When you draw three of them you get your past, present, and future. There are also additional pieces that you may wish to incorporate. These are at the end of the book in their own chapter, and I have included who they are and basically what they do but have left some of the possibilities open for your interpretation. Use these if you wish, or stay with the thirty-six primary pieces. Remember, they are only designated primary or additional at my discretion. You may choose others that align more closely to your requirements and customize your divination parameters as you see fit.

So why would you use this system? That's a question I have been asked often during the time I was developing this. The answer is neither simple nor straightforward. Divination is by its nature curvilinear. A plus B does not always equal C. Even though your fate has been woven into the tapestry of the great hall you still have free will. Whether you take a plane, train, or truck to your destination is up to you. The fact that you are going to arrive at that particular destination is mostly predetermined, but the nuances of the journey are ever changing. And most importantly, only the Norns know what they wove, so you are still capable of determining your own destiny. No one will know if you are following your predetermined path or not, and that's probably the way it should be.

Here is an example: You may be sitting at a café enjoying your latte. This morning you were warned that you would be in danger and that caution was warranted. For some reason, you wait to pay the bill until you wipe your face and throw away the napkin. In that instance the car that would have struck you in the parking lot has moved through its path and out of your circle of influence. You have changed your future by altering your present. Was it something your mother taught you about wiping your mouth before leaving the table in the past that caused your present to alter your future? Was it ever really your fate to die in that parking lot? Which is woven into the great tapestry? Will you ever know? Such is the way of divination. Everything is connected to everything is connected to everything...

Back to the original question of why anyone should use this method. These pieces take into account the personalities of the gods and goddesses as well as the characteristics of their creations. Each piece represents a specific person or thing and those then interact with each other to give you, in my opinion, a better prediction than pulling a single rune stone from a bag. It is important to realize that unlike tarot cards or other divination systems, these pieces are not mirror images of orientation. By that I mean that if the piece is good in one orientation that does not mean the piece is bad in the reverse. Each orientation has a separate meaning with unique characteristics. This may be difficult for those who work with tarot to grasp, but I am certain you can work through this. Since there are three ways to read the piece, a binary good/bad or yes/no is not applicable.

This book also gives a detailed history of the cosmology of the Norse, their beliefs, their customs, lives, loves, and deaths. Each chapter goes into the history of the item being studied and how it came to be. Why is this item more important than any other? Who was this god or what did that hammer or horn do and why? The background to the gods will hopefully give the reader a connection to the piece. It is all well and good to talk about Fenrir and Týr and why one lost a hand to the other. It is better, though, to know who Fenrir was, why Týr lost his hand, what significance the event had on the future of the realms, where the event happened, and how the event was performed. Each chapter answers these six questions: who, what, when, where, why, and how. I recommend that you read the entire book before beginning to use the pieces. That way you will have an idea of what pieces are presented and what is said about each of them.

Divination, as previously stated, comes in many forms. These pieces are but one of them. However, for a Norse practitioner I believe that these pieces will resonate more soundly than tarot cards, rune stones, or bones. The gods are still in Asgard as well as wandering the other eight realms. This divination tool will give you the ability to draw from them and find your own path.

UNDERSTANDING THE ALPHABET

There is much misunderstanding about the "Norse alphabet" of the sagas and *Eddas*. Many that I have spoken to over the years want to read the sagas in the original "Norse." When I try to explain that the sagas were written a few hundred years after the events were told in oral tradition, they are dismayed or left in disbelief. I feel these are the same type of people who think that today's Bible was actually written by John, Paul, and Luke.

To say that something is written in Old Norse is a misnomer since there was no writing other than runes, which were only used for rituals and memorials before the Roman alphabet arrived on the scene. However, the scribes who actually wrote the oldest manuscripts in the twelfth and thirteenth centuries spoke a language virtually unchanged from the language of the first inhabitants to come from Norway in the ninth century. In other words, the spoken language in Iceland didn't change for three hundred years. In that time, the alphabet was Futhark, but it was only used sporadically, and not for writing down more than a few words at a time.

So you cannot say that these Futharks are "Old Norse," although many still say that the sagas are "Old Norse" when in actuality they are written in "Old Icelandic." If the Norse had thought to use the Futharks as a written language it would have been as easy as writing everything out, but they didn't.

They never thought to document their lives and deaths with the Futhark even though they could have.

In an interview with Dr. Andrew Lemons of Clemson University, he pointed out that "whether you say 'Old Norse,' as opposed to 'Old Icelandic' is largely a question of nationality. 'Old Norse,' though standard for most of the twentieth century to mean 'any and all of the mutually intelligible dialects represented in medieval Scandinavian writing,' has been falling out of use for the past few decades because most medieval Scandinavian writing that anyone reads is from Iceland. Moreover, 'Old Norse' sounds a bit like it means 'Old Norwegian' in Scandinavian ears, and therefore Icelanders have always said 'Old Icelandic' (*forníslenzk*) to mean what foreign scholars (and everyone else) have been calling 'Old Norse.'"[3]

Therefore, there are two alphabets in play here used to represent several mutually intelligible North Germanic dialects. The first alphabet, the Futharks, were used for notes, monuments, and magical ceremonies. There is some graffiti in the Middle East that is Futhark as well as many memorial stones placed throughout Scandinavia attesting to the courage of certain warriors or lineage. The identifications of the pieces in this book are given in Futhark because I liked the way they looked. However, they could just as well have been written in modern English.

The second alphabet is the actual written alphabet of the sagas and the *Eddas*. That's the alphabet of the twelfth- and thirteenth-century Icelandic poets and writers that I wrote about earlier. This early written alphabet more closely resembles the Icelandic alphabet of today. And, while the dialects of spoken Norse—whether Old Norwegian or Old Icelandic—share many cultural similarities, the written language of the sagas is unmistakably early or Old Icelandic.

There are many books on the Futharks, so I will not go into more detail here. Suffice it to say that the Futharks are one alphabet and the Icelandic, adapted from the Roman, is another. It's the Icelandic that I want to further explain.

There are thirty-two letters in the Old Icelandic language, twenty-six in the English alphabet. But some of the letters we use in English, they don't use

---

3. Dr. Andrew Lemons, private conversation, Clemson University, April 18, 2020.

in Icelandic. And some of the letters we use have multiple versions in their alphabet. Let me explain.

Early Icelandic used twenty-three Roman or runic letters, most shared by the contemporary English alphabet, during the time of Snorri Sturluson, who wrote many of the poems and prose of the gods. The c, q, and w have never been part of their internal lettering system. Although the z is no longer used today, it was used in medieval times. However, the Icelandic alphabet does still use these four letters when writing words from other languages such as English, German, etc.

In addition, there are six variations of some letters and four medieval letters that are still in use. The six letters that are variations are: á, é, í, ó, ú, and ŷ. In other words, all the vowels have alternate letters. The other four letters are: ð, þ, æ, and ö, although the ö is a modern representation of the hooked o that looks like this: ǫ. To make matters more interesting, some of the medieval manuscripts also use the letters ø and œ. However, to keep from scaring most of you, these are the thirty-two letters that you will see used in this book when dealing with names, places, and things. You will also see them used when lists are alphabetical. The alternate vowels will come directly after the non-stressed vowel. The ð, called eth, an alternate of d, will come right after that letter. The þ, as we said earlier, is called thorn, æ is named æsc, and then the umlaut ö. They all come at the end of the alphabet after z in the medieval alphabet and the stressed ŷ in the current alphabet.[4]

Below I have included a chart of the Icelandic letters and their names.

Letter	Name	Letter	Name	Letter	Name
Aa	a	Íí	í	Tt	té
Áá	á	Jj	joð	Uu	u
Bb	bé	Kk	ká	Úú	ú
Dd	dé	Ll	ell	Vv	vaff
Ðð	eð	Mm	emm	Xx	ex
Ee	e	Nn	enn	Yy	ufsilon y
Letter	Name	Letter	Name	Letter	Name

---

4. Stefán Einarsson, *Icelandic: Grammar, Texts, Glossary* (Baltimore and London: John Hopkins University Press, 1945), 1.

Letter	Name	Letter	Name	Letter	Name
Éé	é	Oo	o	Ýý	ufsilon ý
Ff	eff	Óó	ó	Þþ	þorn
Gg	ge	Pp	pé	Ææ	æ
Hh	há	Rr	err	Öö	ö
Ii	i	Ss	ess	Zz	seta

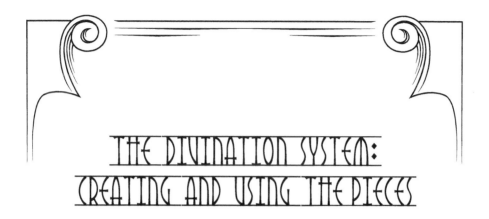

THE DIVINATION SYSTEM: CREATING AND USING THE PIECES

The set of divination pieces is easy to create. You may use cut-out cardboard or poster board. Cut the pieces in squares, circles, octagons, or whatever shape you wish. Use a marker to write what piece it is as the pieces are identified in the chapters, or you may identify your pieces any way you wish when you make them. Draw pictures, use your native language, or go Irish and use Ogham. There is no wrong way to mark your pieces.

If you wish to work with wood, then carve them from dowels or limbs of trees. Cut them out with a saw if you want them a little fancier. If you work with clay or ceramics, make them that way and use a metallic or kiln pen to mark them before firing. My set that I'm currently using is made from a piece of ash that I turned on my lathe and then cut to quarter-inch thicknesses. I sanded both sides and marked one side with a black marking pen. They're not fancy and I'm okay with that. They work for me and have since I created the first set years ago from the limb of a tree in my backyard. In other words, there are a million ways to personalize your set of divination pieces and they don't have to cost you any money.

Let me give you two examples of how to do this.

The first example is the least expensive way possible. Find a piece of cardboard. A cardboard box is perfect, especially if it is plain on both sides. Once you have that, find a quarter. Mark thirty-six pieces and cut them with a pair of scissors or a sharp knife. A modelling knife is perfect. Once you have the pieces cut to round, start with Baldr and work your way through the pieces until you get to Yggdrasil. Copy the signifiers from the book with a marker. When you are finished you have a working set of divination pieces.

Another example would be if you have a wooden dowel. Carefully cut the pieces a quarter of an inch thick or as close as you can without cutting yourself. Gently sand the two sides with sandpaper: start with 120 and go up to 200 grit. Once they are smooth, mark them as you did the paper set. Make certain, though, that the pieces are smooth and flat on both sides so that they may lie flat on your surface that you use to read them.

You may do whatever you wish to make them your own. Some might want to sage them to cleanse them before using. Others may wish to perform a blessing to their particular god or goddess before using. Still others may just want to use them as they are. How you personalize them is up to you.

Once you have your own pieces, you will need something to hold them in. You may have a special box or leather pouch that you want to use. You may want a cloth bag so that you can pull the string tight to keep the pieces in place. You might even use a coffee can or food container. If you are a whisky drinker, there is a Canadian brand that has a lovely blue flannel bag with gold lettering. I always thought that Odin would get a kick out of divination pieces being held in a liquor bag. Whatever you use, make certain that you cannot see the pieces before you take them out and place them on the surface you are reading from.

How to Use the Pieces

Clear your mind of outside influences. Try to think of what you are asking from the pieces and what you want to learn. You may write it down to remember your question or you may vocalize the question out loud. Take a few deep breaths and calm yourself. There is no rush to this. It is between you and the gods.

Once you are ready, pull three pieces one at a time from the container. Take them out parallel to the surface. Be careful to pull them out and place them on the table or wherever you are reading them exactly the way they came from the bag. It's the easiest way to maintain the proper orientation since the piece will be either vert or inverted. If the piece is pulled with the blank side up, then it doesn't matter how you set it on the surface you are using. I refer to this reading placement as "over."

If the piece is pulled with the character side up, look carefully to where the dot is. The dot is at the bottom of the piece. Therefore, if the dot is not above the center of the piece then it is read vert; that is, right side up. If the dot is higher than the center of the piece then it is read inverted, or upside down. If the dot is exactly in the middle of the line then it is read vert. Remember, the default is vert in reading the pieces. In the example above, the piece for Sif on the left is read vert because the dot is below the center line. The piece for Týr on the right is read inverted because that dot is above the center line.

Place each piece on the surface. Once all three are there you may read from the left to right for past, present, future. Each chapter of this book first gives you the background of the piece. It will give you some history of who or what you are dealing with and a basic knowledge of the situation. These short introductions to the pieces are meant to familiarize you with the scenario of each piece. I have always felt it was important to understand the background of the pieces in order to best interpret their meaning. The rest of each chapter gives the three meanings of the pieces. The vert is given first, the invert is given next, and the over is given last. In each of these sections I give a short explanation of what the piece in that orientation means. Then the remainder of the section is further broken down as past, present, and future.

An example of a three-piece draw of past, present, and future might look like this:

This reading is Hel in your past, Baldr inverted for the present, and an over Sleipnir for your future. In this instance Hel in the vert position past is the queen of the dead and the ruler of Helheim. She is the last thing you will see before punishment or glory. She is the end of whatever you are about. In the present is Baldr inverted. Baldr inverted is sacrifice. There is great loss or grief in your present situation that must be contended with. However, the over Sleipnir is strength in battle and winning against overwhelming odds and conflicts.

Therefore, if this was your reading I would tell you that in your past you have lost greatly and many things of importance have been taken or stripped from you or you have had to give them away. Currently you are undergoing a period of great sacrifice that you feel may be too much or too overwhelming. It could be death, destruction, loss of love, freedom, money, whatever, but in the end, with Sleipnir you will overcome all adversity and conquer.

The more you use the pieces, the better you will connect with them. And after reading the short introductions of the gods and creations, you may wish to know more. Use this book as a grimoire. Write in it. Use it for notes. Scribble in the margins. I have always worried about people who had perfect and pristine books in their library. I wondered if they were ever read.

Pieces by Name and with Signifiers

Angrboða   Auðhumla   Balder   Bifröst   Bragi

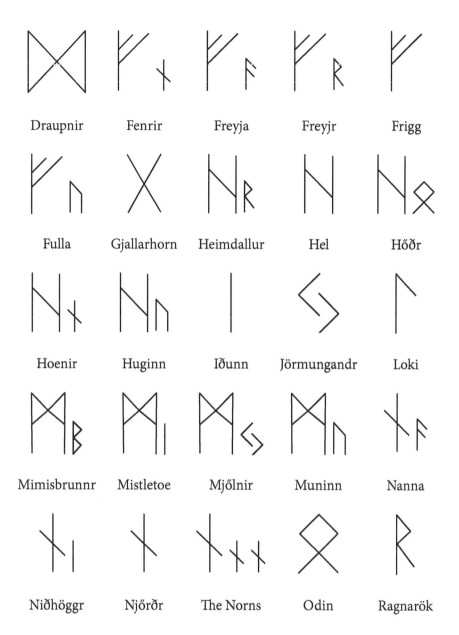

Draupnir	Fenrir	Freyja	Freyjr	Frigg
Fulla	Gjallarhorn	Heimdallur	Hel	Höðr
Hoenir	Huginn	Iðunn	Jörmungandr	Loki
Mimisbrunnr	Mistletoe	Mjölnir	Muninn	Nanna
Niðhöggr	Njörðr	The Norns	Odin	Ragnarök

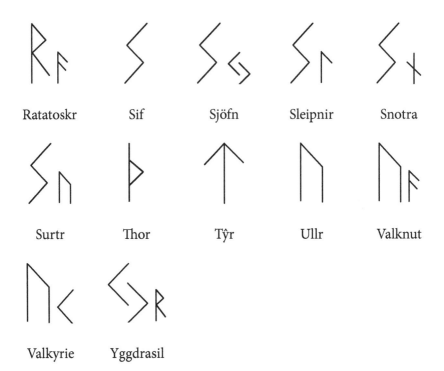

| Ratatoskr | Sif | Sjöfn | Sleipnir | Snotra |

| Surtr | Thor | Týr | Ullr | Valknut |

| Valkyrie | Yggdrasil |

THE BEGINNING AND THE END

No creation story makes any sense. It doesn't matter what religion you follow or what path you take. It's all faith. And the Norse creation of the nine realms is no different. With that in mind, I'm going to tell you a story.

How It All Began

In the beginning there was Ginnungagap, the chaos between the realm of fire called Muspelheim and the realm of ice called Niflheim. In the realm of Muspelheim lived Surtr the fire giant. No one knows when or where he first originated from but at that point in time he was the king of Muspelheim. Between these two realms grew a great mass of ice.

Over the next millennia more frost from Niflheim and fire from Muspelheim travelled across the great cosmic void of Ginnungagap until they clashed at the mass of ice in an elemental disruption. As the heat and cold met, the steam coalesced into the giant Ymir. Ymir was the father and mother of all other giants. He was also capable of birthing giants from between his legs and through the sweat of his armpits.[5]

---

5. Karl E. H. Seigfried, ed., *The Illustrated Völuspá: The Prophecy of the Seeress* (Nashville: Fateful Signs, 2018), 11.

As more ice melted from the heat of Muspelheim, a great cow named Auðhumla came forth. The great cow fed Ymir with milk from her udders and she began to lick the salt from the ice for nourishment. From the ice that Auðhumla licked was first seen a head. As the great cow licked more a torso was revealed. And then the legs and feet. Finally the great being that was neither giant nor cow was born. His name was Buri and he was the first of the Æsir.

Buri had a son named Bor.[6] There is no record of who he had a son with but at this point the only other options were giantesses. Bor then had three sons with the giantess Bestla: Odin, Vili, and Ve. Odin eventually took control of everything and became the leader of the Æsir and king of Asgard, but at this point there is only he, his brothers, his father, his grandfather, and a lot of giants that are still being created from the orifices of Ymir.

Odin sees the problem with the void being overwhelmed with giants and he and his brothers kill Ymir. From the corpse of the great giant the three created everything else. Draining the blood from the corpse they created the oceans; however, the blood flowed so quickly from the body that it swept away Auðhumla and all but two of the giants who escaped in a makeshift boat. These two giants, Bergelmir and his wife, went to Niflheim where they began a new race of ice giants.

Ymir's skin and muscles were ground up to become the soil beneath their feet, at times called the firmament. His hair was used to create the plants and once his brain was removed his skull was used as the sky and the brain matter became clouds.

As Odin and his brothers fine-tuned their creation, they took the sparks from the fires around them to create stars. After the bones were exposed by creating soil they made the mountains. Maggots that emerged from the rotting body of the great Ymir were turned into dwarves. Four of these dwarves were tasked to hold up the four corners of great Ymir's skull, thus keeping the sky above us all. Odin named them Nordi, Sudri, Austri, and Vestri. Today the Icelandic for these directions is Norður, Suður, Austur, and Vestur. Some things don't change much over the millenia, although I feel that these names were appropriations of the Norse or Icelandic as Snorri Sturluson and Saxo Grammaticus were writing down the cosmology of the Norse.

---

6. Seigfried, ed., *The Illustrated Völuspá*, 12.

Once the landscape and cosmos were finished, Odin and some friends created the first two humans. There are great gaps in the creation of the nine realms in the literature and much of what we know was written down hundreds of years after first being told so there is a degree of faith that goes with much of this story. Odin gave the two humans soul, Hoenir gave them heat, and Lothur, who might have been Loki in this instance, gave them "a goodly hue."[7] They were Askr and Embla, also known later as Ash and Elm.[8] These two began propagating the world of Midgard that we know as Earth with other humans. The sun and moon were already in existence but there was no one to drive the chariots that pulled them across the sky; they just pulled themselves. At that time a human called Mundilfari named his two children Sol and Mani, meaning Sun and Moon.[9] The gods were so enraged that a human would dare compare his children to their creations that Odin cast the two into the sky to drive the chariots around the world. Chasing these two chariots are the children of a giant, in the form of wolves named Skoll and Hati Hrodvitnisson. These two wolves will eventually overtake Sol and Mani at Ragnarök and consume them, thrusting the world back into darkness.[10] At the same time Odin cast two more giants, Nat and her son Dag, into the sky to follow each other as night and day.

Once all this was accomplished, no one rested. Yggdrasil was set into place as the world tree that connected all nine realms. Yggdrasil is a great ash tree. So great, in fact, that it spans the entire cosmos from Asgard at its crown to Niflheim and Jotunheim at its roots. At each of these three realms there is a stream that feeds the great tree.

The first stream or well is in Asgard. There is Urðr's Well where the gods meet in discussion.[11] It is also at this stream that the Norns sit and weave the tapestry of each individual into the great hall and from the waters nourish Yggdrasil.[12] It is at Urðr's Well that Odin hung for nine days on Yggdrasil to gain the knowledge of the runes.

---

7. Seigfried, ed., *The Illustrated Völuspá*, 35.

8. Seigfried, ed., *The Illustrated Völuspá*, 32.

9. Seigfried, ed., *The Illustrated Völuspá*, 15.

10. Seigfried, ed., *The Illustrated Völuspá*, 76.

11. Seigfried, ed., *The Illustrated Völuspá*, 19.

12. Seigfried, ed., *The Illustrated Völuspá*, 39.

The second stream or well is at the base of Yggdrasil in Jotunheim. Here at Mimisbrunnr, also referred to as Mimir's Well, Odin sought the knowledge of Mimir. When he arrived at the stream Mimir would not let the All Father drink of the water until he sacrificed one of his eyes for a drink. Odin therefore plucked his eye out and gained the knowledge of Mimisbrunnr. It was this knowledge that brought the All Father both happiness and despair, for he saw all that was to come all the way to Ragnarök, the end of their days, and the destruction of the nine realms as he knew them.

It is Mimir's head that Odin talks to and receives knowledge from. During the Æsir-Vanir war, Hoenir and Mimir were sent as hostages to Vanaheim. Hoenir was supposedly the smartest of the gods and when in the company of Mimir did indeed show exceptional intelligence. However, when Mimir was not present, the Vanir realized that Hoenir was incapable of decision or thought. In anger, the Vanir decapitated Mimir and sent his head back to the Æsir. Odin kept the head viable using a combination of herbs and magical spells and carries the head with him for guidance.[13]

The third and last stream is in Niflheim at the Well of Hvergelmir. This stream is fed by the dripping waters off the horns of the magical stag Eikthyrnir, who is perched atop of Valhalla.

There is much life in Yggdrasil. At the very top is a great unnamed eagle. No one has been able to decide why the eagle is unnamed since everything else in the cosmos has a name, but no one seems to know what his is. And between his eyes sits a hawk named Veðrfölnir.[14] Why a hawk should sit between the eyes of an unnamed eagle is another mystery never explained in the stories and that the hawk should have a name but the eagle is without one mentioned is a tale that is yet to be told. At the roots of the tree is the serpent Niðhöggr, who chews at the roots and eats the dead corpses of those who go to Helheim. These two are bitter enemies and are kept bated by the squirrel Ratatoskr who insults both at the expense of the other up and down the tree, day in and day out, until Ragnarök.

---

13. Seigfried, ed., *The Illustrated Völuspá*, 91.
14. Jesse Byock, trans., *The Prose Edda: Norse Mythology*, by Snorri Sturluson (London: Penguin, 2005), 26.

Where It All Happens: The Nine Realms

No one has ever been able to logically explain the placement of the nine realms in Norse cosmology. These nine worlds are interconnected to the great tree Yggdrasil. As we just explained, the tree is fed by three water sources at its roots. Niflheim and Jotunheim are usually placed at the bottom of the great tree since roots are at the base of a tree, and the third water source of the great tree is Urðarbrunnr in Asgard. Therefore, the root that is in Asgard is at the crown of the tree since Asgard is said to be above Midgard and Midgard is in the center of the nine realms.[15] The illustration on the next page is as accurate as possible considering that the realms are not placed on a two-dimensional plane but are located around the limbs of the great tree.

Seven of the realms end in "heim" and two end in "gard." Midgard and Asgard are the only realms that end in "gard." All the other realms end in "heim," or "home of." This goes back to a basic tenet of the Norse where there is safety and there is danger. Asgard is considered innangarðr. That is a place of safety and security. The home of the gods is the most secure of the realms. Midgard, however, is what the gods see as the best humans may attain. It is also a place of safety with high walls and rules to govern and where the gods wander through to keep their presence known. All the other worlds are a form of útangarðr. They are wilder and less predictable. They are dangerous to those who are not from there, but they are also untamed lands where fortunes may be made, fame gained, and battles to save the realms fought.[16]

Asgard

Asgard is the home of the Æsir. This is the race of Odin, Frigg, and the other gods of the Norse world. At the end of this section there is a family tree of the prominent gods and goddesses of the Æsir. Asgard is a great world, but not as densely populated as one might expect. Each god or goddess has their own hall, and the great hall, Valhalla, is also located here. Asgard is connected to Midgard by Bifröst and is guarded by Heimdallur. From his great hall Odin sends out his two ravens, Muninn and Huginn (Memory and Thought), to

---

15. *"Midgard,"* Online Etymology Dictionary, Douglas Harper, accessed 5/24/2020, https://www.etymonline.com/word/Midgard.

16. Kirsten Hastrup, *Culture and History in Medieval Iceland: An Anthropological Analysis of Structure and Change* (Oxford: Oxford University Press, 1985), 143.

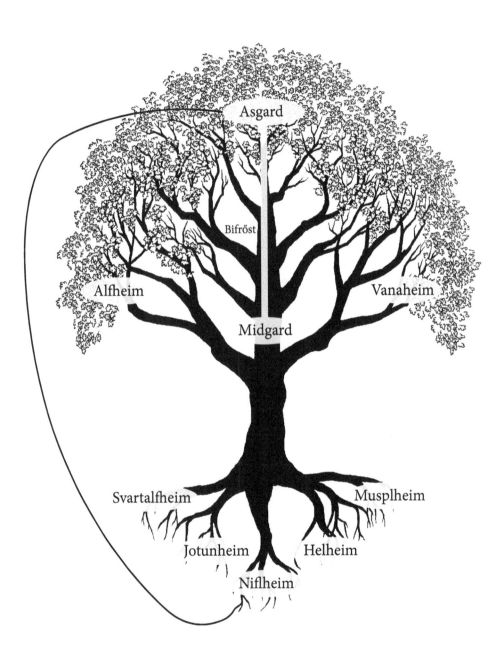

fly over Midgard and bring him news every day of what is happening in the realm of the humans. When Odin travels, he is often seen or perceived as an old man with an eye patch, a wide-brimmed black hat, and a spear. He has his two ravens on his shoulders for companionship. You might see him and then look and he is gone. Such is the way of the All Father. There but not.

Vanaheim

Vanaheim is the realm of the Vanir. These beings are similar to those in Asgard and were at war with the Æsir until a truce and hostage trade was arranged. While Asgard is a more organized world, being of *innangarðr*, Vanaheim is less civilized, being of *útangarðr*. It is the home of Freyjr and Freyja, the god and goddess of the earth, the hearth, the crops, and the fields.

Midgard

The world of humans is Midgard. Here the gods watch over us and at times interact with us. We are the only realm that is connected by Bifröst, which leads me to believe that the other realms are traversable through other means and Midgard can only connect to Asgard. I believe that Bifröst may be seen in the north on cold nights when the sky is clear and the elements are right. Others call this phenomenon the aurora borealis. Who is to say which of us are correct?

Midgard is encircled by a great wall called Miðgarðr and was created from the eyelashes of the great giant Ymir for our protection more than for the other realms. Around the landmasses are the great seas, and in that sea Jörmungandr strangles the world as he bites his own tail. At Ragnarök all the world of Midgard will be destroyed in fire except two humans, Líf and Lífþrasir, who will hide in Hoddmímir's Wood and emerge to repopulate the new realm. It is uncertain whether this wood is a kenning for Yggdrasil since no location of this wood is given.[17]

---

17. Carolyne Larrington, trans., "Vafthrudnir's Sayings," 45–1, *The Poetic Edda*, Oxford World's Classics (London: Oxford Press, 1996), 47.

Alfheim

There are three worlds that are above Midgard: Asgard, Vanaheim, and Alfheim. In the cosmological order of importance these three are substantially more "civilized" than the others, even though by the name it is considered útangarðr. Alfheim is the home of the light elves and is ruled over by Freyjr, even though he is neither an elf nor from Alfheim. Little is known of Alfheim.

Muspelheim

Muspelheim is the home of the fire giants ruled over by Surtr. Muspelheim was there at the beginning of creation and will be present at Ragnarök. It is a world of fire and smoke. Surtr shall leave Muspelheim at Ragnarök and with his great sword of light and his fire giants, Eldjotnar, destroy all that is.

Jotunheim

Even though Jotunheim is the home of the frost giants and usually at war with Asgard over something or other, there seems to be a lot of interaction between the Jotnar and the Æsir. Jotunheim is a cold and desolate place but not as cold and desolate as Niflheim. The Jotnar, or Jotun depending on whether you are speaking of many or one, live in a great city called Útgarðr and are ruled by King Thrym. One of the roots of Yggdrasil runs into Jotunheim to Mimisbrunnr. The giant Þjazi who lived in Þrymheimr and kidnapped Iðunn lives in Jotunheim. Even though Loki is given the title of god he is actually a Jotun and the son of Fárbauti and Laufey.

The Jotnar have a tense relationship with the gods of Asgard and they are in constant conflict with Thor. It is interesting that Loki as a Jotun is so connected to the Asgardian god of thunder while being one of the instigators of Ragnarök and most of the chaos that happens.

Niflheim

Niflheim is one of the first of the realms. Here the cold and ice nourishes Yggdrasil at Hvergelmir. Here also the great serpent Niðhöggr chews at the roots of the great ash. Few live in Niflheim and it will remain a cold and desolate place far after Ragnarök.

Svartalfheim

Svartalfheim is also called Nidavellir. It is the home of the dark elves, those we refer to as dwarves.[18] Their world is riddled with tunnels and catacombs where fires burn eternally and the forges of the smiths work great pieces of art. Some of the works the dwarves fabricated that we know of are Thor's hammer, Mjölnir; Skidbladnir, Freyjr's magic ship; Gleipnir, the magical rope that keeps Fenrir at bay; Draupnir, the ring that creates other rings every nine days; Odin's spear, Gungnir, which never misses its target; Brísingamen, the necklace worn by Freyja that cost her four nights of sexual pleasure; and Sif's long golden locks after Loki cut off her real hair.

Helheim

The last realm is that of the dead. In *Grimnismál*, Helheim is said to be at the well that feeds Yggdrasil.[19] If that is the case then Helheim is located somewhere in Niflheim, but I believe it is its own realm. I believe that Helheim is a realm separate from the others. When Hermoðr rode to Helheim to ask Hel for the release of Baldr, Hermoðr rode Sleipnir for nine nights until he reached Gjallarbú, the bridge that spanned the river Gjöll. There Móðguðr, the giantess maiden who guarded the bridge, asked Hermoðr what his reason was for crossing the bridge. He told her he was sent from Odin to seek the release of Baldr from Hel. After that he rode until he came to the gates that kept the dead in and others out. Jumping over the gate he rode to the palace of Hel.[20] A journey of nine nights, a river to cross, and a gate to jump over places Helheim far enough away from Asgard to be its own realm.

Wherever Helheim is—and it is most likely at the base of Yggdrasil, closest to Niflheim—it is where the dead go. Those who are not accepted into either Folkvang or Valhalla are kept in Helheim. However, life after death is not always sorrow and torture. Those who died and were not accepted to Valhalla nor Folkvang live much the life they did while alive. They work, fight, eat, sleep, and prepare for Ragnarök. Those who lived good lives but had the unfortunate fate to die in their sleep or of old age or by accident spend their

---

18. Seigfried, ed., *The Illustrated Völuspá*, 71.

19. Larrington, trans., "Grimnir's Sayings," 31–3, *The Poetic Edda*, 56.

20. Larrington, trans., "Baldr's Dreams," 3–4, *The Poetic Edda*, 243.

afterlife in a different level of Helheim than those who were thieves, murderers, or oath breakers. They are, though, all destined to fight for Hel against the slain warriors of Odin at Ragnarök.

The Races

It would seem to some that there are only two races of beings in the nine realms since you mostly hear about the Æsir, the gods of Asgard, and their continual fight with the giants of either Jotunheim, Muspelheim, or Niflheim. And to be honest these two races do take up a lot of real estate in the sagas and stories, but they are not the only ones present. Humans play an integral role in the nine realms because without them there would be no one to tell the stories. It was the medieval mythographers and historians, Snorri and Saxo basically, that made the gods and other beings what they were.

Also, when you read the sagas it always seemed to me growing up that the giants were much larger, uglier, meaner, and deadlier than the gods. They were the size of mountains when Thor tried to kill them, or they could create such havoc that they must have been terrifying. But then you read about the gods marrying the giants and extolling their virtues and beauty above all others. So what is the real story of these races and who were they? I wrote a bit about them in the realms section but here let me describe them better and give a more accurate genealogy for those who want to know.

The Æsir are the actual gods. While they're not really gods, they're close enough and we're the ones making the determinations. The Æsir were created when Auðhumla licked the first one from the great ice block that floated somewhere between Muspelheim and Niflheim. The male Æsir were muscular, tall, and great warriors. They lived for adventure and often went looking for trouble so that their fame would grow. The female Æsir were beyond compare in their beauty. Most had long blond hair and radiant features. They were in constant demand for marriage and the giants seemed especially obsessed with them.

Even though by the second generation of the Æsir they were already part giant, no one seems to take that into consideration. They fear and hate the giants while at the same time taking them into their homes as mates, friends, confidants, and assistants. It's a strange relationship at best and you can see the intermixture of the races in the charts that follow.

The Vanir are also called gods. They are much the same as the Æsir in stature and again mix and mate with the other races frequently. It's almost as though the Vanir and the Æsir were cousins that didn't quite get along one holiday and decided to fight it out before the next big meal. While the Æsir live in Asgard, the Vanir live next door in Vanaheim. As we discussed earlier, Asgard was innangarðr while Vanaheim was útangarðr. So Asgard had the better lawn and landscape and Vanaheim didn't.

Next we have the humans. In the time of the sagas the men and women were shorter, stouter, and less lithe than they are now. They lived a harsh existence and died young, often in either childbirth or battle, depending on your gender. While the Vanir and the Æsir could and did comingle their genes, sex between humans and the other realms seems to be, if not forbidden, then at least frowned upon. Little is stated in the sagas as to whether the humans shared bed and bread with the gods. Bread yes, but seldom if ever bed even though these three races looked basically identical.

Now come the giants. In the literature these creatures are described as being of immense size and stature. They are the size of mountains and Thor sleeps in one of their gloves to give an idea of the scale of these beings. However, when Freyjr sees Gerðr he thinks she is the most beautiful creature he has ever seen. He immediately gives away his sword to Skirnir, thus removing his most valued weapon at Ragnarök. If Gerðr is the size of a mountain and a vile creature, then how is Freyjr able to fall in love with her for her beauty, woo her, and love her as a mere Æsir?

I believe that these size differences are constructions of the writers Saxo, Snorri, and others to create a disconnect between what is perceived and what is. I believe that these are literary tools to add to the mystery of the stories. In reality giants are no larger, darker, or more dangerous than the Vanir or the Æsir. And obviously they are just as desirable.

The fifth race are the dwarves. In modern times we have seen dwarves portrayed as short, hairy, ugly little creatures that live in caves and make things of metal. However, nowhere does it state in the sagas that the dwarves are short, hairy, or ugly. They are described as darker and referred to as "dark elves" when their realm of Svartalfheim is referenced. They are also obviously masculine enough to be acceptable to Freyja when she sleeps with four of them to gain Brisingamen; although, as Loki states, Freyja has slept with almost everyone including her brother, Freyjr.

And since they are called "dark" or "darker elves," does that mean that they are the same build and stature as elves, just of a darker hue? Do the elves of Alfheim look any different than the Vanir or the Jotnar? I believe it is safe to say that in the actual sagas all the races are similar enough to be acceptable to each other. They may be hated or loved singularly or in groups, but they are nonetheless equivalent in nature.

Who's Who

Below are two charts to give you a better idea of who is related to whom. In the charts the | denotes a child or children of those directly above. ---- is a connection by marriage or sexual contact. ———— are siblings.

How It All Ends

Every beginning must have an ending, and even though this ending ushers in a new beginning, it is only part of the cosmology of the Norse. Every being in the nine realms knew how they were to end. Gods would fight monsters. Friends would fight friends. And in the end the world that everyone knew would be destroyed, only to be made new again.

Æsir

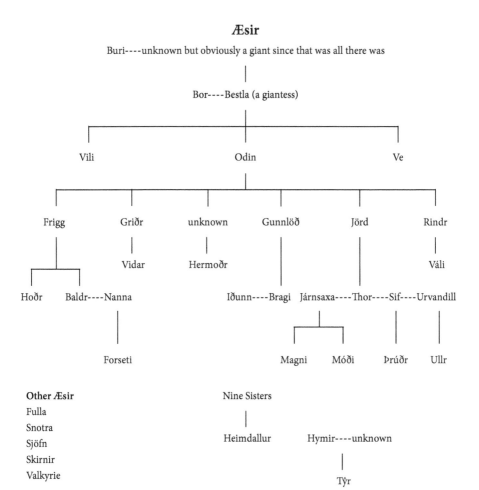

Buri----unknown but obviously a giant since that was all there was

Bor----Bestla (a giantess)

Vili   Odin   Ve

Frigg   Griðr   unknown   Gunnlöð   Jörd   Rindr

Vidar   Hermoðr   Váli

Hoðr   Baldr----Nanna   Iðunn----Bragi   Járnsaxa----Thor----Sif----Urvandill

Forseti   Magni   Móði   Þrúðr   Ullr

Other Æsir   Nine Sisters
Fulla
Snotra   Heimdallur   Hymir----unknown
Sjöfn
Skirnir   Týr
Valkyrie

Giants

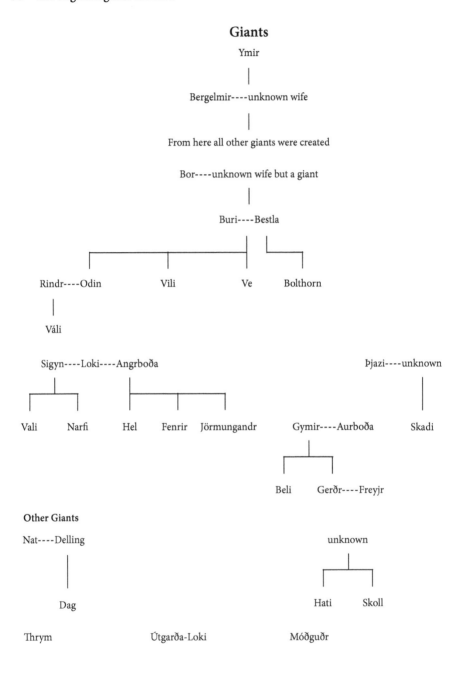

Ragnarök

Ragnarök will be preceded by three years of winter. During this time, darkness and cold will descend upon the lands. Brothers will kill each other for food and the worlds will be thrown into chaos. The two wolves Skoll and Hati will finally catch the sun and the moon, and the world will be cast into utter darkness.

At the appointed time, Fenrir will break his bonds; Jörmungandr will release its tail and shake Midgard, warning of the approaching destruction. Loki will lead the dead through the gates of Helheim and cross Bifröst. Heimdallur will blow Gjallarhorn and the gods and warriors of Asgard and Folkvang will rush forth to fight and die in glorious battle.

With the shaking of Midgard by Jörmungandr, the boat Naglfar, which is made of the nails of the dead, will be released from its ropes and carry the giants toward Asgard. Even though Odin knows the outcome of this battle, he will nonetheless seek guidance from Mimir's head.[21] It is foretold what is to happen and all are playing their part in the preordained theatrical play of death and destruction.

Odin will fight Fenrir and be swallowed by the great wolf. Odin's son Viðar, wearing a magical shoe made from all the leather scraps of all the leather shoes of all the cobblers in the world, will attack Fenrir and with the magic shoe hold the great wolf's gaping maw open to allow Viðar to kill the wolf.

Garm, a wolf of Hel, will kill Týr only to die at Týr's blade. Thor will seek out his adversary Jörmungandr. Thor will kill the serpent but will stagger nine steps away from the carcass before dying of the venom that fell on him. Freyjr will fight the fire giant Surtr but without his sword will die from his wounds. Loki will kill Heimdallur and will die next to him but not until he sees his handiwork come to fruition: that being the end of the worlds and the survival of his daughter Hel. In the end Surtr will reduce Asgard and Midgard to ash and smoke.

---

21. Seigfried, ed., *The Illustrated Völuspá*, 91.

A New Beginning

That's the end of the story, but there is a beginning too. Baldr will return from Helheim, and he and Höðr survive the battles.[22] The sons of Thor will inherit Mjölnir; Njörðr will go back to Vanaheim, where he will mourn the dead. Lífþrasir and Líf will emerge from Hoddmímir's Wood and repopulate the world with humans. It will be the second age of the gods and they will meet at Idavoll to move forward.

22. Seigfried, ed., *The Illustrated Völuspá*, 112.

Part Two

INTRODUCTION TO THE PIECES

There are thirty-six pieces in this divination set. Each piece is unique to the cosmos and cosmology of the Norse pantheon. If you have never heard of these gods or items before then take this time to read the explanations of them. Think of what it must have taken for the early Norse to tell these stories late at night as the cold wind blew across the snowy tundra.

While many think of the Norse as bloodthirsty Vikings, these simple farmers and fishermen were first and foremost family men and women who raised children, took care of the elderly, prayed to their gods, and practiced their religion. They eked out a meager livelihood in a harsh environment where the only guarantee in life was death. To these people the gods didn't offer salvation; they offered a different scenario for the same activities. There people would live to fight, and then after death they would continue to fight and feast until Ragnarök. Enjoy the stories as I have presented them and see the gods as they are: no better or worse than us.

Primary Entities

There are thirty-six primary entities. These entities are gods, other beings, and items that are significant to the gods or the sagas. These are the thirty-six pieces I have been working with for the past twenty years, but I realized when writing this book that some of the other individuals and items in the Norse pantheon may be more specifically suited to you. Therefore, I have other gods and beings listed at the end of the book in the chapter "Additional Entities." There I listed what the piece does in its three permutations. From there you can figure out where you wish to go with them.

It is important to emphasize again that there is not a reverse correlation to these pieces. Just because a piece in vert is good does not mean that the piece inverted is bad. The meanings of the pieces evolved over years to be the way they are presented. Much of their attributes are taken from the personality of the god, person, or entity, but the way they worked themselves into those situations is a product of years of study. I hope this helps if you were looking for a rationale for the pieces and their meanings.

There are nine permutations to every piece. Three in over, three in inverted, and three in vert. In each of those the choices are past, present, and future. The past is everything up to the very moment you are existing right now. By the time you read that sentence it was in the past. The present is the now. People talk about living in the now but that is always happening whether you plan it or not. There is no other place to live but the now. The future is everything from the present forward in time. However, this is where it gets sticky. By the time you get to the future it's still the present. Let me give you an example.

Tuesday morning you have a meeting. It is now Monday afternoon. The meeting is in the future. We good so far? But you can't do anything in the future. You can only action things in the present, so if you are going to cancel it or change it then it is done in the present and that alters the future.

And even though the meeting is in the future, by the time Tuesday morning comes you are now in the present, so the future was never really achieved. That is why I say throughout this book that the future is never reached. It is always the carrot on a stick being held in front of us.

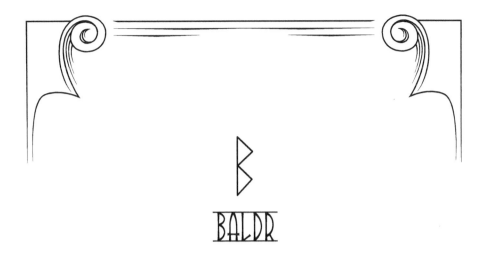

BALDR

Baldr is the son of Odin and Frigg. The most beautiful of all the gods, he was the brother of Höðr and half-brother to Thor. When Baldr reached adulthood, he began to have nightmares of his death. They were so vivid that he sought out his mother, Frigg, to discuss them and she in her wisdom knew that it was a foretelling of the future since she knew all.

Frigg asked all creatures and beings great or small, living or dead, to protect her son since he was the chosen god and the most beautiful of all in Asgard.[23] As she went about the nine realms, she ignored the simple mistletoe since the mistletoe was a parasitic plant that lived off the energies of other plants. Being hemiparasitic (the mistletoe removes food and water from the host plant, not harming the plant enough to kill it but enough to be detrimental to its optimum growth and longevity), Frigg thought that the plant was too insignificant to be of any danger to her son.

---

23. Seigfried, ed., *The Illustrated Völuspá*, 63.

Once Frigg returned to Asgard, Baldr was set upon by all the gods in an attempt to harm him for fun. All forms of weaponry bounced off the most beautiful of the gods and he enjoyed good fortune and health. Unfortunately, as Loki heard of this competition to see who could harm Baldr, he took the mistletoe and fashioned a dart from it. Handing the dart to Baldr's blind brother, Höðr, the god threw the dart at his brother, piercing his heart and killing him. There was so much sorrow and outrage that Odin organized the death of Höðr in retaliation for the deed.[24]

Odin in his despair sent his servant Hermoðr to the goddess Hel to ask for his son back from Helheim. The goddess Hel replied that if every creature and being in the nine realms would mourn for Baldr then she would return the god to Asgard. While in Helheim Baldr and his wife, Nanna, who was cremated with him on his ship pyre, sent back gifts to Asgard to show that Hermoðr had indeed spoken to Hel and Baldr. Nanna sent back a wrap of Frigg's that she had worn while being burned on the pyre and a ring for Fulla, and Baldr sent back his magical ring Draupnir for Odin. Upon Hermoðr's return and report, all creatures alive or dead did indeed mourn for Baldr and wish him back from Hel, with the exception of an old giantess by the name of Þökk. This giantess refused to ask for the life of Baldr back and the goddess Hel kept the slain god in Helheim. It was later discovered that Þökk was Loki in disguise.

This refusal, coupled with the initial death of Baldr at Loki's hand, although through Höðr's action, enraged Odin so greatly that he pursued and eventually captured Loki.

Vert

In the vert position Baldr is the epitome of beauty, love, and acceptance. He can do no wrong and everyone loves him. He is safe from dangers and enjoys the comradery of all those around him.

In the past position the vert Baldr piece is a place of honor and a bright future. The piece gives promise to the reader and you have enjoyed that promise throughout your past. Many love and respect you, but there is a hid-

---

24. Seigfried, ed., *The Illustrated Völuspá*, 64.

den one that you know nothing about who wishes to do you harm. You were wary but there was nothing you could do at the time.

Vert in the present position places the reader in the best of all worlds. Everyone loves you and you can do no wrong. Nothing may affect you and whatever you have attempted you have succeeded in. You might say you are coated with a nonstick surface. Or, in more accurate terms, you are bulletproof.

Vert in the future is one of happiness and joy. You will be satisfied with friends, success, and fame. All will join around you and even though some may sling arrows at you they will bounce off and be of no effect. You are safe and will do well.

Inverted

In the inverted position the Baldr piece is one of sacrifice. You have lost something precious to you and it may be as dear as your safety, your hopes, or even your life. Baldr is a great god and was one of infinite love but also one of pain and suffering. This is your lot with the piece inverted.

Past inverted has been hard on you. You come from a place of great suffering and pain. Loss is not unknown to you and many things have been either lost or taken from you. It is possible that you even sacrificed some of your well-being or possessions for others since Baldr was a god of giving as well as joy and happiness.

Present inverted is also hard on you. You have come into a time that has taken its toll. Loss, either actual or metaphoric, is rampant and with that loss your sanity and health are suffering. There is a heaviness around you that all can see, and you sink deeper and deeper in depression that must be shaken off before it is too late.

Future inverted may be dealt with. With knowledge comes action and a plan. You know that sacrifice is coming. You know that something or someone is going to harm you in the future, and you know or will know how to handle that. As the saying goes, "forewarned is forearmed" and that is your mantra when Baldr is in your future inverted.

Over

Baldr in the over position is one of betrayal, secrecy, and jealousy. Loki in the shadows plotted to kill the most beautiful of the gods and enlisted an innocent blind god to do his dirty work.

In the past position the Baldr piece over indicates the extent to which you have been deceived. You may or may not even be aware of the deception or the amount of jealousy, but once the piece is pulled you should look back on your past and those situations affecting your present for clues and indicators. These indicators may be as insignificant as a comment on social media or as severe as threats or plots against you in your health, work, or family. Whatever they are you must find them out and identify them before they wreak havoc on your world.

Baldr over in the present is no better. You are being subjected to lies, threats, innuendos, and all the other negatives that plague the modern man or woman. Your work might suffer. Your relationships may come to an end. Or you may find yourself in a situation that you feel you cannot extricate yourself from. Again, as in the past, you must identify what is happening and with that knowledge should come a plan.

In the future the over piece of Baldr will at least give you time to plan and seek out what is behind the curtains or who is holding knives behind their backs. Be very careful even with those you may think are your friends when this piece is present in the future. No one is who they appear to be and anything or anyone may turn out to be your undoing. However, with this piece you have a warning and that will guide you to a safer future, even if it takes a while and some sacrifice.

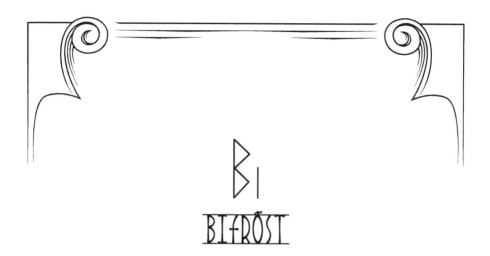

BIFRÖST

Bifröst is the rainbow bridge we all want to cross to get to Valhalla.[25] In the *Poetic Edda* of the thirteenth century, Bifröst is described as a burning rainbow bridge that connects Asgard with Midgard.

To look at the origin of Bifröst, one needs only to look at the northern sky during the winter months in any Scandinavian country. There, shimmering across the stars, is the aurora borealis, a connection between the home of humans and the realm of the gods. It is not hard to understand how the early Norse saw this as a bridge to their final fighting home in Valhalla. And it is not hard to understand the beauty and mystery that still surrounds the bridge even today. Yearly, many go north to see the northern lights. Some are successful and some are not. That's the funny thing about nature and the gods: they don't play by the same rules humans do.

The piece Bifröst is all about connection. Just as the bridge connects our world with the world of the gods, so does this piece connect you to your past,

---

25. Larrington, trans., "Grimnir's Sayings," 44–3, *The Poetic Edda*, 58.

present, and future. Look at it closely when you get it and determine how best to connect those dots.

Vert

In the vert position Bifröst is all about connections. You have them every day in all manners. You connect with your family, your friends, those you work with, and those whom you interact with.

In the past position Bifröst is that connection that you remember. It may be the best or the worst. Whatever it was, look back at it and remember everything about it. Was it good? Was it bad? What did you do to make it either and what was done by others? Could you have changed it if you had acted differently? Never be afraid to admit you erred. And never be afraid to accept that it's your fault.

In the present the connection is ongoing. What are you trying to connect and with whom or with what? How did it begin and how do you expect it to end versus how it may end? Look at all aspects of this. Do not fall into the trap of seeing only what you want to. If you do then you will be grossly disappointed in the future.

In the future your connection is yet to come. Are you anticipating a special connection? Are you willing to take whatever happens? When I was younger, I knew a woman who always asked for a handsome man to love her for the rest of her life. By the time I knew her she had five ex-husbands. I asked her why she limited herself to a specific set of parameters. It took her a long time to understand that a handsome man was not what was in her future. Once she started asking for the love of her life to come to her, she met a woman at work and they have been together for thirty years. Connections are funny like that. You don't always get what you expect but you will usually get what you either need or deserve.

Inverted

While the vert position of Bifröst is connection, the opposite is lost connection. In the inverted position the Bifröst piece is those connections that are lost or broken. There are cautionary tales to be told at this point. Lost or broken connections are also lost opportunities. Study what caused the break and work to avoid them in the present or future.

In the past you've had some slips and falls. You've had good connections and they are now gone. Only you know the situations of these, but be warned not to gloss over them or turn a blind eye to them. Take the blame, if there was any, and the glory, if that was how it ended. Learn from these losses and move forward.

In the present the connections that you have are in great jeopardy unless you have already lost them, in which case they are gone forever. Take care and look twice before you speak or act. Others are looking to you for guidance and wisdom, but it won't take much for them to see that, as the Vanir did to Hoenir, your words are not your own and your ideas are not the worth you think they are. Losses may be curtailed if you act soon enough and accept half of the loss.

In the future inverted position Bifröst is going to play havoc with your world. Everything you have done and everything you are working on will be suspect and you will have to fight twice as hard to keep everything connected. It can be done but it won't be done by sitting at home and hoping. You must get out into the world and act. Take decisive measures with those things you can control and guard against those which you cannot.

Over

Connections may not only be lost but missed. In the over position the Bifröst piece is that missed connection. You may do everything in your power to work your magic and connect or break connections as you need, but some connections are just not there for you.

In the past the connections that you missed are lost chances. To say that "It's all good" is to say "I don't care." A missed connection is a missed opportunity to make or break yourself. Glory, fame, happiness, and heartbreak cannot happen until there is a connection. These things may or may not be pleasant or what you wish, but they are the essential parts and without them you are lost. Look hard at what you missed and work to correct those in the present and future.

In the present you are missing a lot in the world. Bifröst over is your wake-up call to look around you and see what is going on immediately in your vicinity. Don't be lax or put it off until tomorrow because tomorrow never comes. Tomorrow is always the day after today no matter how long you wait. Make the present count.

But in the future there is hope. Tomorrow may never come but eventually all tomorrows become today and then just as quickly become yesterday. If you have a Bifröst in over future then you have connections that are getting ready to happen. If you do nothing then they will pass you by and you will regret the loss. They say, "Seize the day." The future is that day to seize.

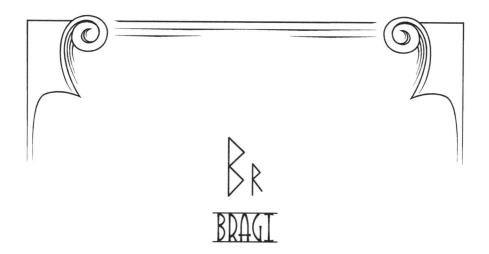

BRAGI

What we know of the god Bragi is limited. He is the son of Odin and the giantess Gunnlöð. Gunnlöð was the giantess that Odin slept with for three nights in order to receive three sips of the mead of poetry. Bragi is married to Iðunn, who kept the Æsir ever youthful with her magic fruit. He is reported to be of great ability with words and song and some claim that he had runes engraved on his tongue that gave him powers that even the other gods did not have in the way of influencing men and women.[26]

Bragi is also credited with entertaining the slain warriors in Valhalla but that may also be an oversimplification of his role of court poet. It would be unfair to say that he was relegated to the position of court jester, but troubadour might be a better description of his talents.

It is possible that Bragi only became the god of poetry after the introduction of Christianity. Little evidence exists that Bragi was known before the

---

26. Larrington, trans., "Lay of Sigrdrifr," 16–1, *The Poetic Edda*, 169.

writings of the Christian monks of the sagas and the legends of the Norse. Either way, Bragi is the poet of the gods and we shall treat him as such here.

Vert

In the vert position Bragi is the entertainer. He is responsible for merriment and song as well as poetry and information. He has a silver tongue and can liven any party or gathering with his presence. When Bragi is in the vert position there is much happiness and joy. Conversation flows and free thought and ideas are abundant.

In the past position you have had a good amount of entertainment. You were the life of the party, knowing the right people and telling the right stories. You were sought out for your knowledge of the situation and how you manipulated people to do your bidding.

Present finds the vert Bragi in a similar position. You are still the life of the party. Wherever you go you are sought out and your council is requested. Your stories are always the best, you are never without a song or a poem, and you enthrall everyone that you meet. You can do no wrong in large groups or private settings.

Future Bragi will find you succeeding in whatever you attempt. You must place yourself in the center of the activity where your engraved tongue will reign supreme. Spend your present preparing for your future if Bragi is in the future position. Learn new stories, listen to others so you may embellish their tales to greater heights, and learn who has the "right" parties and gatherings so that you may rise above all the other noise in the room.

Inverted

In the inverted position Bragi is the dealer with the dead. He is the entertainer of those who have died in battle and those who are in need of solace and direction. As the poet in Valhalla, Bragi entertains the *einherjar*, those warriors who have died in battle and now prepare for Ragnarök at the end of times. His is the most important of functions. These great warriors fight all day preparing for the final conflict and at night they are kept amused and entertained by the silver tongue of the court poet.

Bragi in the past inverted is a position of welcoming yet detachment. You have had a hard time but have gotten through it with words of hope and encouragement. You may have even been the one who had the words for someone else or have acted as a grief or disaster counselor for those who have lost loved ones.

Bragi in the present finds the reader in the situation of being the one who is welcoming to someone else. You have the function of assisting those who need help or with loss or grief. If you find yourself in this state, then know that everything will work out if you remember that the joy you bring others through your words and actions will ripple through their life to others. To say you might be saving a life would be hubris, but it is a noble occupation to be the bringer of joy and happiness to those who need it.

Finally, Bragi in the future gives you the chance to move to an occupation or function where you are more than the sum of your parts. Your words and actions have a cumulative effect on those who need it, and you may be the difference between life and death. Take classes, learn lessons, and practice your craft so when the time is right those who need you the most will regale your deeds and songs for generations.

Over

When Bragi is drawn over there is much misunderstanding. What is said is not relayed correctly. You are misrepresented, your words are taken out of context, and your ideas are erroneously presented. Be aware that all may be taken poorly when the over piece is pulled. While it is not as serious as some other pieces in the bag, Bragi over may lead to many disagreements or situations that could have been avoided.

Bragi over in the past is a disaster that has happened. Whatever you said or presented was taken wrongly and you were blamed or unfairly punished. Everything you tried, failed, and you might have been ostracized for the effort. However, the past is the past and cannot be changed. You must accept what was done and move forward with or without malice toward those responsible. That choice to retaliate is always yours; however, look very closely at what that retaliation may cause.

Bragi in the present over has placed you in a situation that you may still extricate yourself from. Somewhere recently something you said was misinterpreted and you are still feeling the ramifications of that action. Look to your immediate past to resolve your immediate present. Some things cannot be fixed but knowledge is everything, especially when Bragi is in the present and things are still active against you.

Bragi in the future is the best of the over positions. You know what is about to happen. You must be very careful of what you say and to whom. Refrain from random storytelling or elaboration of others' tales. Double-check your data, know your sources, and rely on your wits and your common sense to get you through. As in any situation, the future may be changed with a simple word or a simple deed. With Bragi in that position, that word or deed is paramount and you must be ever diligent to know the difference between praise and prose.

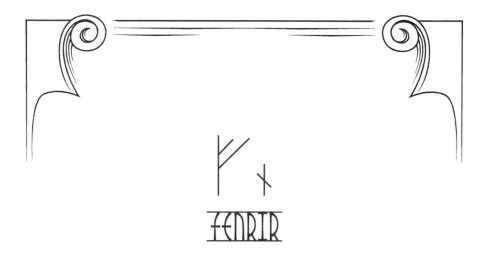

FENRIR

Fenrir is the brother of Jörmungandr and Hel. His parents are both giants, but Loki and Angrboða at least look humanoid whereas Fenrir is a great wolf. When he was born it was foretold that he would be there at Ragnarök. Therefore the gods took the cub to Asgard to raise him and keep him confined for the safety of the worlds.

However, as he grew it became apparent that he would be too great to control soon and a plan was formed to leash him. Creating a game with the great Fenrir, the gods gave him tests of strength that he could easily conquer. Finally, at the appointed time, Gleipnir was presented to the wolf. Whereas the other chains were heavy and bulky, this rope was unnaturally light and airy.

The gods had sent to the dwarves of Svartalfheim a request for a rope that could not be broken. The dwarves created one with six magic ingredients: the spit of a bird, the breath of a fish, the roots of a mountain, the sound of a cat walking, the beard of a woman, and the sinews of a bear.[27]

---

27. Catherine Taylor, ed., *Norse Myths & Tales: Anthology of Classic Tales* (Fulham, United Kingdom: Flame Tree Publishing, 2018), 134.

When Fenrir saw this rope, he instantly became suspicious and demanded that the gods guarantee his release if he could not break the chain as they had guaranteed with the others. When they did that, he further demanded that one of the gods place their hand in the wolf's mouth in the event the gods lied. Only Týr was brave enough to place his hand in the wolf's mouth.

Once the chain was tied around Fenrir's neck he tried and tried to break it. Realizing it was a trick, he bit the hand of Týr, taking it off at the forearm. Then Fenrir was taken to a lonely mountain and lashed to the greatest rock there with a sword in his mouth to keep him from biting anyone else. There the wolf waits for Ragnarök to break his bonds and seek revenge on those who tricked and bound him.

Vert

In the vert position Fenrir is destruction. He is chaos waiting to happen. Even though at the moment he is safely bound in Asgard, he is still just a moment away from Ragnarök. This is the power of the great wolf.

Fenrir in the past is the destruction that has plagued you. You have had hard times and you have had to deal with it. It may have been your fault or it was brought upon you, but either way it was there and it was devastating. What did you learn from those experiences? Did you bring anything forward to the present?

In the present the destruction is all around you. Be aware that it will pass. You are stronger than the storm and you will weather it. You just have to take the reins of your own fate and tie the wolf back to the stone. It may cost you as it did Týr, but in the end you will be rewarded for it.

The future Fenrir warns of cataclysmic events. The wolf will come for you and you must be ready or you will suffer. Fenrir may be killed. It will be done at Ragnarök, although it will take all you have. If you prepare, though, you may weather this storm and come through the other side if not unscathed, then at least unbowed.

Inverted

In the inverted position, Fenrir is darkness. I am not talking about the darkness that is without light; I am talking about the darkness of the soul and the heart. Even though Fenrir was cast into this role by fate, he still had the choice of his actions, to a degree, and those actions caused him to grow dark of heart and being. This is not a positive way to be and one that should be shunned at all costs.

In the past you were in a dark place. It was cold and lonely, and you felt there was no one there for you. Even though you came through that experience and have had better times, those memories still haunt you. The piece in this position reminds you of what it was like then and how numbing it was. Study those painful memories. Don't push them away. Bring them out into the light and let them dissipate like fog in the sun.

The present Fenrir inverted warns that the darkness that is currently around you, whether severe or bearable, will get worse. Only you can mitigate the effect it will have and who will suffer from this. It might get better, but then again, it might not. This darkness could easily go well into the future unless you are willing to work hard in the present to change things. And even that may not be enough.

The future Fenrir is at least a chance to change the way things are going to end. Darkness and cold even at Ragnarök will eventually abate and a new world will emerge. This is how you can approach Fenrir in the future inverted. Usually in the future you are able to thwart whatever is coming through work, knowledge, or planning. Unfortunately, this darkness will come. There is no way to avoid it, but the darkness that will strike you is not permanent. It will take hard work and concentration and most likely the assistance of your closest allies, but you will emerge through the darkness damaged but better for it.

Over

There is much distrust and resentment in Fenrir. To be honest, though, it's pretty much deserved. The wolf was lied to, conned, tricked, and then imprisoned for being what he is: a wolf, albeit a giant one destined to destroy everything in his path. Did the gods expect anything less? He was the son of Loki. He wasn't a poodle. The over position of Fenrir exemplifies this distrust and resentment of all things human and god. Fenrir now lives to kill everything he can when he escapes Gleipnir and wreak havoc at Ragnarök. It's what he was created for, and he has been driven to this end by his surroundings. Could he change and not destroy? He could, but he won't. That is not in his future. In this regard, you might not change either.

In the past the Fenrir piece shows you that at one time you were in a place of great distrust. You were hurt or damaged and it jaded you to others. Hopefully you worked your way through it, or you may still be there, where you trust few, if any, around you. You need to let that go. Distrust, to a degree, is helpful but can be destructive. I'd rather use the word "cautious" instead of "distrustful." I also use the term "preventive" rather than "resentful." This gives me better control over my emotions, and it might help you also while you examine what you have gone through and where you are now.

Present Fenrir over is a warning. If you continue on your path of distrust or resentment you will damage yourself and those around you. Again, be cautious, but paranoid is just around the corner from where you are now. Look hard and long at what is there and why you were hurt. If you were scratched by a cat, that does not mean all cats will scratch you. It also doesn't mean that you must not trust any other cats. This holds true for those who hurt you or do you wrong. That does not mean you should hold that against everyone of that age, race, sex, gender, religion, political opinion, etc. Distance yourself from that person who hurt you, but give all others the benefit of the doubt. Finally, whatever you do, do it with your eyes wide open. Don't let emotions cloud your judgement as you move forward.

In the future you will be hurt again. You will be maligned, slandered, and metaphorically beaten and chained. There is no way to avoid this. It is your fate. But there is a way to mitigate the damage that will be done. Surround yourself with those who know you as a fine and goodly person. Keep them close to you so that when the damage and accusations are cast your way, your friends and admirers are there as your shield wall. You will still be damaged, but the end result will be lessened and you will recover quickly.

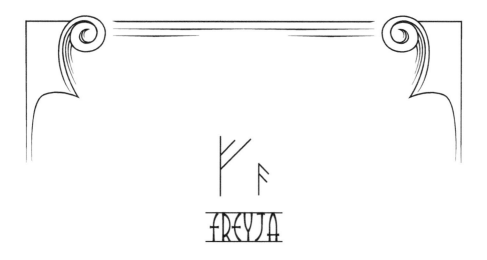

FREYJA

Freyja is the goddess of beauty, fertility, precious metals, and magic, specifically seiðr. She is the twin sister of Freyjr and together they make up much of what we know about the gods in the sagas. While most of the other gods and goddesses are Æsir, the twins are Vanir. However, they have been in Asgard so long that most dedicates of the goddess forget that detail and treat her as an Asgardian of Æsirean lineage.

Freyja came to be in Asgard as part of the peace agreement arising from the Æsir-Vanir war. The war began when Freyja visited Asgard and, as she was a practitioner of seiðr, many of the Asgardians wanted that knowledge. To that end they did whatever they could to learn the magic of the Vanir and in so doing turned their back on what made them gods and role models to others.

Since they were incapable of taking responsibility for their own shortcomings, they blamed Freyja for what they ultimately did and tried to murder her. In fact, they attempted to murder her three times, but each time she was reborn again from the debris of the flames.[28] As these attempts to kill the most beautiful of the goddesses continued, each side began to fear and hate the other until all-out war broke out. As the war raged, each side realized that war was not the answer and ultimately each side sought peace.

Surprisingly, the peace they sought involved sending hostages to the other side and the Vanir sent Freyja, Freyjr, and their father, Njörðr. I find it interesting that the cause of the war was Freyja living in Asgard and now she was to live there as a peace tribute indefinitely. And as she lived there, she, her brother, and their father eventually became official Æsirean and their Vanir past was lost to the poets.

Freyja is not just the goddess of magic. She is also the goddess of love, and to that end takes her love to a heightened degree. She is easily distracted, so to speak, even though she is married to Óðr, who, it is said, "went away on long journeys," leaving Freyja alone to figure out what or whom to do next.[29] While in Asgard one day she went to the forge of the dwarves in Svartalfheim and spied four dwarves creating the most beautiful necklace she had ever seen. Wishing this necklace for herself she tried to purchase it with gold and silver. Instead, the four dwarves Alfrik, Berling, Dvalinn, and Grer told Freyja that if she spent a night with each of them, they would gift her the necklace. She did, and that's how she obtained the necklace Brísingamen and Freyja's reputation as somewhat of a free-loving spirit came to be.

However, Freyja is also the goddess of the Valkyrie and they in turn bring the slain to her hall, Folkvang, as well as Odin's hall, Valhalla. While there is no tangible evidence of what goes on at Folkvang, I hazard a guess that since Freyja is surrounded by cats, precious metals, and excessive love, these three areas are well-represented within the hall. Finally, Freyja is a goddess of art and she is the muse to the painters, writers, sculptors, and builders in all nine realms. Where there is creativity, Freyja is there, if not in person then in spirit. Other than Brísingamen, Freyja's other great possession is her cloak of falcon feathers that allows her, or the wearer since Loki has borrowed it in the past, to fly in the guise of a falcon.

---

28. Seigfried, ed., *The Illustrated Völuspá*, 40.

29. Seigfried, ed., *The Illustrated Völuspá*, 48.

Vert

When the Freyja piece is pulled in the vert position, Freyja is the chief of the Valkyries and the honor maiden of the dead. She welcomes the dead to her hall and serves them as is her want. She shares the dead with Odin, and in that regard is equal to the All Father for the fallen.

In the past a vert Freyja piece shows that you have dealt with death and dying. Those around you have been lost and you are at a loss yourself to understand how to deal with that. Loss and grief are parts of living, and to that end you have made it through, scarred and broken perhaps, but still here in the present. For that, be thankful to the goddess.

In the present the Freyja vert piece is more bad news. You have death around you, but you also have honor at the end of the ordeal and a golden hall to go to; therefore, you may take power from that and prepare your future.

In the future you must look out for loss and grief. Be extra vigilant against dangers that may appear or are just around the corner. As with many of the future piece readings, forewarned is forearmed.

Inverted

Inverted the Freyja piece is love and beauty. There is much about Freyja to admire, from her long golden hair, her perfect (well, at times) demeanor, to her magical abilities. Freyja brings love wherever she goes and passes that love around in ample measure.

The past inverted shows your great love of all things and the beauty that abounds around you. There could have been joy and happiness but there may also have been jealousy of your beauty or your love for others. It is a two-edged sword of love and beauty. Those who have it want to keep it and those who don't will do anything to obtain it. Similar to the gods longing for the magic Freyja had in Asgard, so, too, will mortals fight and die for the love and beauty they feel they so richly desire.

The present inverted is much a continuation of the past love and beauty. Be wary of what lies about you in your day-to-day life, for love and beauty are not always appreciated nor valued. If you do have love or beauty, then treasure it as a gem but not as a possession to hoard. Those who value love or beauty above all else soon learn that they have lost both.

Inverted future Freyja gives you a glimpse into where you have yet to go. Your love is overwhelming, but take care that it is not overburdening. Your beauty will be a thing to behold but in the reverse of that you may become a thing of ugliness while thinking you are beautiful. Remember, love and beauty are not in your eyes but in the eyes and arms of those around you. Seek out those who need your love and make them beautiful in others' eyes.

Over

Freyja has a reputation as an easy woman. That is being kind in verbiage. She was known to have slept with almost everyone in Asgard and was reputed to have even slept with her brother, Freyjr. What is certain, however, is that while married she willingly offered herself to the four dwarves in exchange for the necklace Brísingamen. While this is only one example, it is a striking one that goes to the heart of Freyja as a lover of, well, love.

Freyja in the over past is one of known lust and satisfaction. Your life has been measured by your carnal knowledge, and even if it was not of your own doing it is still there. Take responsibility for what has happened, or if the lust or love was thrust upon you against your will, admit that it happened, seek justice through legal means, and do the best you can to move through it. The past is the past and acceptance of your baser instincts is essential.

The over present piece is your situation currently. You may be in love or lust with someone that gives that great feeling in return. You may be in love and it is unrequited. You may be loved and you do not feel the same. Whatever the situation, the love that surrounds you is ever present and you must deal with it, accept it, and plan to utilize the best of it and eliminate the worst of it.

The future over Freyja is a world that is yours for the taking. Using what you are capable of and giving what is freely given and accepted, you will cut a swath through the world around you. However, on the opposite side of that is the dark and seamy side of love where everything has a price and everything has a cost—not always the same thing. Be very careful of where and to whom you cast your net and offer your love. This is a dangerous world and there are many out there who would take your innocent offerings and turn them tawdry with their ill thoughts and actions.

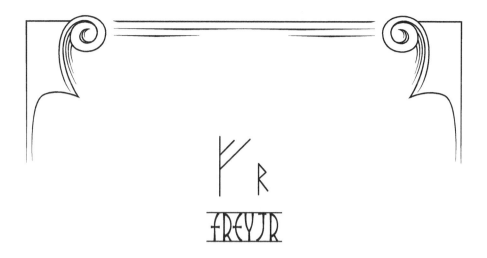

FREYJR

Freyjr is the brother of Freyja and the son of Njörðr. He was offered up as a peace hostage after the Æsir-Vanir war and became an honorary citizen of Asgard. Freyjr is responsible for the harvest, and when crops are planted or reaped, thanks are given to this blond-headed god. Freyjr is also the god of fertility of the earth, which goes along with his harvest responsibilities.

Although Freyjr was born in Vanaheim and is an honorary Asgardian, he lives in Alfheim with the elves. Statues of Freyjr are often shown with a significantly large penis to represent his role as the fertility god of the earth. While the penis is an affectation of fertility of the earth, it is also taken as a personal affectation, and many pray to the god when they are looking to start a family or are having difficulty reproducing.

Among Freyjr's possessions are his sailing ship Skíðblaðnir, which is said to be able to be folded up to fit into a pocket of the god's cloak and will always have a favorable wind. This makes sense since his father is Njörðr, the god of the sea and maritime activities. Also, Freyjr either owns or is accompanied by—depending on your interpretation of animal familiars—his boar, Gull-inbursti. On land, Freyjr's transportation is a chariot pulled by boars, although it is never stated if Gullinbursti is one of those. It is interesting to note that each sibling, Freyjr and Freyja, both have their selective animals draw their chariots—Freyja's being pulled by her cats.

At Ragnarök, Freyjr will die at the hands of Surtr. This death will come about because Freyjr gave away his beloved sword to Skirnir during his quest and courtship of the giantess Gerðr, whom he eventually married.

Freyjr is mentioned in many of the Icelandic sagas and his followers are characters in more than a few of Snorri's stories. Some of the more popular ones are *Völuspá*, *Grimnismál*, *Lokasenna*, *Skirnismál*, and *Ynglinga*.

Vert

The Freyjr piece in the vert position is one of growing and expanding. The harvest, children, family matters are all within the power of Freyjr to enhance. Whatever the piece touches will succeed and you will have abundance in all matters.

In the past the vert piece is success and great joy. Your fields were over-flowing with crops and your family prospered. Children were healthy if there were children, and if you wished for some or more of them, they were provided. Your council was sought after in the fields of husbandry and horticulture and everyone looked at you as the shining success.

Your present is everything you wanted it to be. There is no downside to this and you are doing well, even if you don't know it. I have found that success is oftentimes missed because we look for it in conventional ways and often overlook what nature sends us. Gaze around you to your family and friends. How are they benefiting from you and yours? Do you show them the love and compassion that you are getting from the land around you? Are you happy with what you have, or are you looking for something that is not there? The end of the rainbow is said to have a pot of gold, but not everyone wants or needs a pot of gold. What is it that makes you happy? Freyjr is there for you if you are open to seeing it.

Freyjr gives you a great and glorious future in this permutation. Be cogni-zant of what you want and plan to get it. You have the tools and the expertise to accomplish whatever you set your mind to. You just need to trust yourself and your surroundings. Be careful, though, of taking too much for granted. Just because you have Freyjr on your side and in your fields and bedroom does not mean you can become lax or lose focus. Continue to practice safe procedures, take few to no risks, research all your decisions before acting, and you will be successful.

Inverted

Inverted Freyjr is the restrictive. The piece represents contracting and removing of all things beneficial. It is the failure of the crops, the barrenness of the mother, or the death of the dream. When Freyjr is contracted, nothing works properly and the earth itself suffers.

Inverted in the past is the loss of whatever was going on for you. It could have been your fortunes, your love, or your bounty—either actual or metaphoric. The loss may be slight or it may be significant. Whatever the case or the severity, the contracting of the situation leads to desolation and despair.

Inverted in the present shows Freyjr still actively affecting your well-being. You may have had a good past, but in the present things are not working out the way you had planned. Be aware that things can always get worse and that situations may be put in place to alleviate these discomforts, but they may be more than you are willing to pay. Look for the causes of these discomforts and alleviate them. Change your habits, rotate your crops, or rotate your livestock.

In the future inverted Freyjr may be altered or eliminated altogether. You know what is coming. You know that your livelihood is in jeopardy and you must do something to alter the situation. Before you attempt to work around the situation, though, make certain that you have all the facts and all the tools at your disposal. Seek guidance from others if necessary, and look to those who have had similar situations and have ridden them out successfully. It does no one any good to reinvent the wheel when someone else already has one to lend you.

Over

The over piece for Freyjr is one of cold, desolation, and winter. This is the opposite of the bright and successful piece of vert. You are in a time of slumber. Your crops have been harvested, your pigs and cattle have been slaughtered, and your fields are plowed under until spring. Take this time to inventory your losses and gains. Write your ledgers. Contact your kith and kin and start your seedlings in anticipation of spring.

Over past Freyjr has given you little and taken much. The winter has been difficult on your hof (a common word for hearth or home), and you scrambled to get a grip on what was left. Look deeply into what you have left and what you must get in order to progress into the next phase, which is the present. It may not all be serious, though. Your fields are dormant, but they may not have been destroyed. Your crops are in the bins, but they have been well-tended and you have enough for the winter. Your livestock may be barren this year but not all dead. Not everything is death and destruction.

Present over finds Freyjr in a slow and steady state of mind. Be aware that things will slow down and stop. You are at a point where you must make a decision to either continue your path or abandon it. If you choose to continue, the wait can be long and arduous. There will be hurdles in your immediate future but there may be sunshine and abundant yields. But if you choose poorly, your hof will suffer and your life will too. Know that all depends on you and you are the only one who can weather this storm into the future. Plan now so that you don't have to later.

The future over is a better place to be. The harsh winter has passed and you are looking at a milder spring. Even though it will be difficult to recoup your losses, you are able to overcome the hardships and at least break even in the immediate year. After that depends on you and how you handle adversity. If you have the strength of Thor, then you will be fine. If you buckle under the pressure and fail to rise to the occasion, then you will be less than fine. I was going to say destroyed but that's too fatalistic. You are not there…yet…so let's not think about that. Go with the strength of Thor and press on.

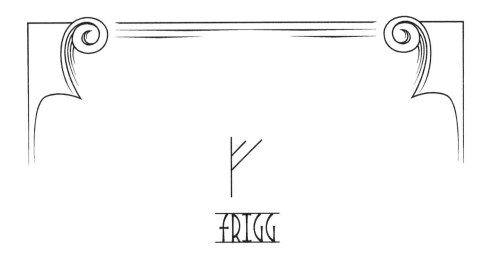

FRIGG

As a member of the Æsir, Frigg is a goddess of Asgard and the wife of Odin. In Old Norse sagas and scripts she is also referred to as Fulla, but that is still contested by some linguists, and in the poem *Grimnismál* both Frigg and Fulla are mentioned as two separate individuals.[30] Also hotly contested is whether in early Norse history Frigg and Freyja were the same goddess that later became separated as the myths and legends moved farther north into Scandinavia.[31] Friday is named for her.

Although she is Odin's wife, she lives in her own hall of Fensalir where she takes guests and holds her own counsel. As a völva she is involved in seiðr, which is the divination of the fates (not to be confused with the Norns, who are often referred to as the Norse Fates by those who are not well versed in the history of the gods).

---

30. Larrington, trans., *The Poetic Edda*, 51.

31. Stephan Grundy, "Freyja and Frigg," in *The Concept of the Goddess*, ed. Sandra Billington and Miranda Green (London: Routledge, 1998), 55–57.

It is fitting that Frigg would be the wife and consort of Odin since she, like her husband, has the gift of prophesy and the future—although Odin paid dearly for his gift and Frigg, it seems, was born with hers. One example in the *Lokasenna* is when Loki berates Frigg for practicing sorcery, and Freyja quiets Loki by reminding the trickster that Frigg, as the goddess of prophesy and sight, knows the death of everyone. At that point Loki changes his subject matter and eventually leaves the hall.[32]

Although Odin has many children by many sources, Frigg has two sons by the All Father: Baldr and the blind god Höðr. Through trickery by Loki, Baldr is killed by his brother Höðr, which leads to the beginning of the end of the gods through the chase of Loki and his ultimate imprisonment.

Vert

When the piece is pulled vert, Frigg is the All Mother. She is nurturing, caring, and benevolent to all. She is portrayed as the wish bringer and the healer. She may also be seen as the seer or sorceress in her role as a practitioner of seiðr.

In the past this piece represents motherhood and the hope for the future. You have known the future and have acted upon it. There is wisdom in your actions and you have performed for the betterment of those around you and yourself. Whatever you have done in the past will reflect upon the present, so be aware of your actions and take heed and council to avoid missteps.

In the present the piece may be read as all-knowing, even though you may not want to accept what you know to be true or evident. You can see where you need to go and what you need to do to get there. The cost may be too much but that is the way the present often is.

And in the future this piece is the culmination of all things harmonious and benevolent. You will be successful, knowledgeable of that around you and in the future. Further, you may understand the nuances of the future and how to exploit that knowledge for your success.

---

32. Larrington, trans., *The Poetic Edda*, 89.

Inverted

The inverted piece of Frigg is the home mother. Here the piece represents her solidity as the hearth mother, the loving mother, and the grieving mother for those lost to her. She is representative of all the positive aspects of the hof, where food, drink, and safety are ever present.

This piece in the past is the happy childhood, the loving parent, the doting mother. It represents all that is longed for with rose-colored glasses at times, but still the image is positive and beneficial.

In the present the piece shows that you are in or at a positive and safe space. No harm may befall you while in the hof, and when trouble may come knocking, the All Mother is there to protect you and drive away the wolf from the door.

In the future this is the best outcome to be hoped for. Happiness, peace, comfort; all are parts of the All Mother's offerings from her gilded hall of Fensalir.

In the presence of Odin you may experience unexpected changes since the All Father has ideas of his own. Further, Baldr in the inverted past may cause a delay of those positive things due to grief and loss. Add a significant amount of time to the process of the present. No definition of significance is given at this time.

Over

When the piece is pulled in the over configuration, Frigg is the vengeful matriarch. In this position the All Mother is angry and dangerous. She is grief-stricken and will lash out at whatever is closest to her.

In the past position you have had a hard time, been deceived or debased and fought for justice or revenge—often neither successfully. There is a cruelty to you and your enemies, as well as your friends, were victim to that side of your nature. There is knowledge to your viciousness and when it was unleashed it was all-consuming and unabated.

In the present situation this piece is the personification of hate and anger. You know what is to come and you don't care. Anyone or anything in your path is subject to your wrath, and if that destroys you as well, then so be it. Self-destruction is possible if it means achieving your objective of revenge.

Take heed if this is your piece because there is no going back from this path once it is begun.

In the future position you are in a dark place. Whatever time it takes to crawl out of your hole will depend on you and you alone. Find whatever happiness you may and cling to that during your time in darkness and light may eventually appear. However, you may never recover if you allow the goddess to take you too far away from the light.

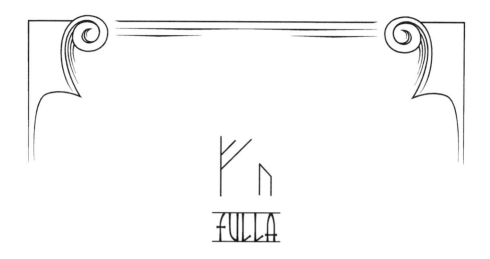

FULLA

Fulla is an interesting goddess. At times she is given the identity of Frigg, at other times she is the personification of Freyja, and others claim she is a servant, maid, confidant, sister, or friend of Frigg. Given that this goddess is so well versed at being something else gives an idea of what she actually can accomplish.

Fulla in reality is the handmaiden and best friend of the All Mother, Frigg. She is credited by High, the lowest of the three kings in the *Edda Gylfaginning*, as being the fifth most important Æsir in the pantheon. High along with the other two kings, Just as High and Third, are together really Odin in disguise and, therefore, they would know who is considered most important in Asgard.[33] Fulla is said to be a virgin, which would preclude her from being Freyja. Fulla also is given the job of taking care of Frigg's footwear but most importantly Frigg's secrets. Fulla is the confidant of the mother goddess and knows all but tells nothing. Finally, Fulla is instrumental in healing animals; in

---

33. Anthony Faulkes, ed., *Two Versions of Snorra Edda from the 17th Century*, 2 vols. (Reykjavik: Stofnun Árna Magnússonar, 1979), 188–190.

the Merseburg Incantations of the tenth century she is said to heal a wounded mare.[34]

Vert

Fulla in the vert position is one of assistance. Fulla is the helpful maiden who is there for you when you need it. She embodies everything that is good and pure about help and caring. No sacrifice is too great for Fulla in this position.

In the past vert Fulla is the epitome of caring and helpfulness. She is there to take care of you or to take care of whomever needs her, and you have done that in your life. You may have been the dutiful son or daughter to a parent, or the parent to a child. You may have rescued someone and nursed them back to health or you might even have saved lives in a profession that routinely does that. Your life is one of giving and for that you are well looked at. However, the other side to this is that you may have been looked down on as being subservient or too helpful. Jealous people will come up with all sorts of ideas for those whom they perceive as too nice or too good. Balance is the key to this piece and the position.

Carrying that over to the present, the piece may be said to be the same as the past: caring and helpful. Remember balance in your life. It is wonderful to be caring and helpful but to overextend yourself, or to extend yourself in places or with people that are not of that mindset, may be hazardous to your well-being. If the Fulla piece in the vert position comes up in your present, then look to see whom you are caring for and why you are caring. Do not cease the action, merely understand what the driving force is behind the deed. Remember, seek nothing for your aid no matter who says differently.

Vert Fulla in the future is the best of the vert positions. You are going to be needed, and unlike the past and present where you may have already done something that has angered or enflamed someone else, you now know what to look out for and what to avoid. Place yourself in positions that will do the most good with the least amount of drama and turmoil. It is the best advice anyone can give at this moment.

---

34. John Lindow, *Norse Mythology: A Guide to the Gods, Heroes, Rituals, and Beliefs* (Oxford University Press, 2001), 227.

Inverted

Fulla inverted is her secretive side. As the confidant to Frigg the All Mother, Fulla knows all the secrets there are in the great halls. And she tells none. This is the power of Fulla. She is the eyes and ears of Frigg, and when something needs to be done or advice needs to be given, it is Fulla who is tasked.

Fulla inverted in the past finds you knowing too much and not being able to discharge that information. If knowledge really is power, then you have all of it but nowhere to use it. You could have been a loyal friend or a trusted ally in the past. However, just as easily, your past could be filled with intrigue that has put you in a dangerous situation. They say that once someone tells anyone a secret it is no longer a secret. This is the best advice you may get for your past. Deal with what you have done or what you have not and move into the present as best you can.

The present, though, is not without its dangers as well. In this position Fulla is one of assistance but not without compromise. Secrets are neither welcomed nor appreciated if they are not complementary. Keep your counsel close and your mouth shut. Whatever you may think you know is much more valuable if you know it and you keep it where it is supposed to be. Honor those who trusted you with this information and they will trust you again. If you have broken that trust then it will take a long time, if ever, to regain it.

Fulla in the future inverted warrants caution. You will be told something or given something that is powerful and not necessarily safe. If you can refuse the information then do so. Nothing good will come of this. However, if you are thrust into a situation where you cannot escape, then extricate yourself as quickly as possible with your eyes wide open and your lips sealed.

Over

The Fulla piece in the over position is one of healing of livestock and other animals. Fulla is not just the handmaiden of the All Mother. She is in her own right a powerful goddess who was prayed to for help and guidance on the farm and in the hof.

Fulla in the past shows where you have been in regard to your animals. You are a great lover of all nonhuman living things. You often take in strays and would take in more if you could, but at times your past situations have not allowed that. Be content that you have lived a good life with those around you and continue to be there for those who cannot fight back. However, if you are not of a temperament to assist animals in need, then this is your wake-up call. Fulla in the past gives you a chance to change your ways and better yourself before the end finds you without friends or allies.

In the present Fulla over gives you an idea of what is possible with what you have now. You are in a position to make a decision that could be life-altering and it involves some species of animal. You may be thinking of changing your profession, purchasing a hof, or moving to the country. Any of these are possible with Fulla in your present position.

Fulla over in the future is where you want to be. You see yourself surrounded by nature in a peaceful and pastoral setting. Harmony abounds, and with the knowledge of Fulla and her assistance you will make a good choice and find that perfect fit you are looking for.

Note: If you find Fulla in the present and Freyjr in the future (or the other way around), then you are definitely going to be looking at farm life and the harvest of both crops and animals as your livelihood. Be assured that it is the right choice and move with certainty to your goal.

GJALLARHORN

Gjallarhorn is the horn of Heimdallur. He is destined to blow this horn at the advent of Ragnarök to warn all the realms of the oncoming danger of Loki and his minions.[35] Gjallarhorn was first used at Mimisbrunnr to drink from the sacred waters of the well. By doing so, the god Heimdallur gained the wisdom and knowledge that allows him to monitor everything and be the eyes and ears of the gods while standing watch at Bifröst.

Vert

When the horn is in the vert position it is one of warning. As Heimdallur blows Gjallarhorn at Ragnarök so does this piece warn you on past, present, or upcoming dangers. Take these warnings to heart and pay attention to what was warned about and how they transpired.

In the past position Gjallarhorn is your warning horn. You may or may not have known that, but either way you were warned that there was danger

---

35. Seigfried, ed., *The Illustrated Völuspá*, 88.

and either you did something about it or you didn't. It's too late either way, but at least you know that if you believe you were warned then you were right.

Present Gjallarhorn vert is your chance to do something about the warning. As Heimdallur warns the gods at Ragnarök so, too, are you being warned that trouble is coming. Whether the trouble is from inside your circle of associates or from outside of your influence, the warning is real and the danger is significant. Take care and be careful.

In the future you will face dangers that you are not prepared for. Nothing you do will suffice to curtail the dangers, but at least the warning will arrive soon enough that you may seek assistance from others. Rally your forces and prepare for battle, and I don't mean figuratively. This is not a metaphor; this is an actual battle of wits or brawn. Your safety and very life are in the balance. Be aware of that and act accordingly.

Inverted

Heimdallur drank the waters of Mimisbrunnr from Gjallarhorn. In the inverted position Gjallarhorn is that vessel to prepare you for whatever lies ahead for you. Take that preparation seriously. These are troubled times, and you must deal with them forcefully and directly.

Inverted past has Gjallarhorn giving you the tools necessary to repair everything that is broken before the past becomes the present. It also allows you to see where you needed to go and what helped you get there. Just because the past is gone does not mean it's been forgotten. Remember these preparations as you move forward and take these measures with you.

However, in the present the Gjallarhorn piece is the opposite of what you would expect for preparation. There is no preparation. You will be completely unprepared for what is about to happen. You have let your guard down and the giants are coming with no warning. If you are lucky enough you may have some inkling of what to do and whom to do it with; however, you will have to move quickly once you understand how unprepared you are. The lessons you should have learned, you ignored, and the steps you should have taken, you didn't. This is not the best time for you.

In the future the Gjallarhorn piece makes you the ultimate prepper. You have everything you will ever need for any situation. You have stocked your larder, your stores are filled, and your skills are honed. There is nothing that you are not prepared for, and that gives you the edge in the future. Others will look to you for guidance and you will have it to offer. You will be the horn in the distance alerting all others of their ill preparedness and they will thank you for it.

Over

It is too late. The giants are already at the door. Gjallarhorn over is the ultimate warning and understanding that the end is about to happen and the best you can do is to accept that and fight on even if there is no chance of winning. Although this sounds like the end, it isn't. It is, though, a harsh reality for you to learn. Even Ragnarök is not the end. And this will not be the end either—just another chance to begin again.

In the past the Gjallarhorn piece is your wake-up call to the things that are looming. You didn't even know they were there, but they have been amassing for some time at the periphery of your vision and now they are prepared to strike.

The present Gjallarhorn gives you little opportunity to prepare for the battle. You have been lax, and it has shown in your demeanor and your preparedness. Now the enemy is at your gate and you are scrambling before it is too late. I hate to tell you, but it's already too late. Whatever this battle is, you are going to lose it due to your failure to prepare. It won't be the end of the world, as Ragnarök is, but it will be serious enough to degrade you and those around you for some time.

The future holds great things for you. Even though the giants are crossing Bifröst you have heard the sound of the horn. You know what to do and you have the tools to accomplish this. Don your armor and go forth into battle ready to do your best. Even if you lose this fight you will win fame and glory, and in the end you will be victorious in the eyes of those who matter.

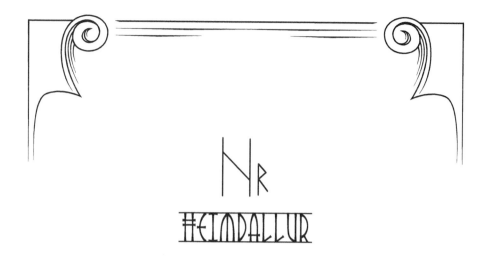

HEIMDALLUR

Heimdallur is the god of the watch. He is the sentry of Asgard and the early warning system of Ragnarök. From his high home, Himinbjörg, he sits at the end of Bifröst where the rainbow bridge enters Asgard. Here he watches the nine realms and all that happens. It is said he can hear grass sprouting and wool growing. His eyes are keener than the great eagle and sharper than all the others combined.

His origin is shrouded in mystery but also in impossibility. He is credited as having nine mothers and one father: Odin. While this may be hyperbole, I believe that it is closer to the truth than you may think. We regularly say of someone that they are a "child of the earth." We mean the individual is of the earth and is "one" with the nuances of our planet: Midgard. I believe that Heimdallur is the child of the nine realms. When we talk of his mothers, we are talking of the nine worlds and how he is the child of each of them.

While he seldom visits Midgard, he does occasionally get there. On one such visit he was instrumental in creating the three classes of the Norse. Dressed as a poor traveler, he first visited a couple in a ramshackle hut on the seashore. He was taken into their hovel and given food and drink. He lay with them and on the third day gave them fire with which they could now cook their food and heat their hut. This couple had a son, and he was the ancestor of the thralls, the lowest of the three classes.

The second couple were farmers who worked with their hands. Heimdallur helped the husband make a loom for his wife and, after lying with them for three days, left them. They had a son, and he was the ancestor of the yeoman farmers. The third couple lived in a fine castle. The husband spent his time hunting and his wife spent hers looking pretty. Heimdallur spent three nights with this couple, and their child was the ancestor of the Jarls.[36]

At Ragnarök Heimdallur will blow Gjallarhorn to waken all the warriors in Valhalla to the onslaught of the giants. During that final conflagration, Loki and Heimdallur will lock in mortal combat and kill each other. However, until that day, Heimdallur watches and listens. He neither gives nor gets counsel from the other gods and, like a statue, he guards. That is his function, and he carries it out perfectly.

Vert

In the vert position the Heimdallur piece is one of guardian. He is the watchman of the gods and through him they are all safe and secure until the final horn blows.

In the past position the vert piece is one of protection. You have been the guardian of many things and they are safer because of you. It may or may not be a duty you chose, but it is a duty you are performing. Only you know whether you are pleased with the success or failure of your occupation, but that is what makes this piece so essential: you are the one who understands the process, and you are the one who must determine whether you are pleased or not with your past.

In the present you have a decision to make. Do you continue to protect that which is in your charge or do you abandon your function? Look closely at what it is you are protecting. Is it a secret? Is it valuable? Is it personal? Any of these may be paramount to your well-being but only if you are willing to deal with it directly. Do not skirt around the issue. Take it head-on and

---

36. Taylor, *Norse Myths & Tales: Anthology of Classic Tales*, 129–130.

address the item you are guarding. Ascertain if it is worth the price you are about to pay. Then live with the decision.

The future vert piece finds you ready to take on a new position. You are being given the opportunity to protect that which is important. What that is, only you will know, and when you get to that point you will know what to do. Do not suffer from the decision you are about to make. Continue as you have, and when the time comes and the item is passed to your care, you will make the correct decision.

Inverted

Inverted the Heimdallur piece is one of all-seeing and all-knowing. There is nothing that escapes you in your quest for the answer to your question. Not only do you know what to say and what to do, but you are also adept as to how to say and do it. Your decisions are golden, and you are looked at in awe for your ability to determine the right course of action for each branch.

Inverted in the past has shown that you acted as the gatekeeper for something that needed your expertise. You did it out of loyalty, but it was still a chore and you are now done with it. Whether or not it was successful only you will know, but your choices were pure and you did what was expected.

In the present, you will discover you have all the answers to everyone's questions. However, before you give them everything they ask for, ask yourself if this is something that they really need to know. Just because they ask and you know does not give you the right to tell them. Not everything is better off known. Remember that.

In the future a decision is coming. Look at all sides before deciding. Too much is at stake for the wrong answer, and even though you know all the questions and all the permutations of the answers, you still have to balance that with the morality of the situation.

Over

Heimdallur in the over position is the end of things. Think of Ragnarök on a smaller, more personal scale. Things are going to happen that will change your world by ending parts of it. Center your mind. Put your affairs in order and know that when you are through this you will be better for it. Ending does not necessarily mean death or destruction. It just means the end of one thing and the beginning of another.

Past over has seen you through some great upheavals. Your world has been rocked and you didn't know if you were going to get through them but you did—possibly scathed and battered but better for the experience. Now that it is over you can take stock of the situation and learn from what you did and what you didn't do. This will assist you in repeating the actions in the future.

In the present the over piece finds you contemplating much change and need for resolution. Things are in upheaval and you must decide which parts are most important and which parts may be cut loose. Remember, just because you feel that everything is important to you at the moment does not mean that everything really is. Eventually everything fades into memory, and this too shall.

Over future is the hardest to deal with. It's coming and you have no idea what it is. There will be actions that must be taken and ramifications that must be dealt with. Endings are coming, and they will come fast and furious. Keep your stance steady and balanced. Everything begins and ends for a reason, even if you don't know what that reason is at the moment.

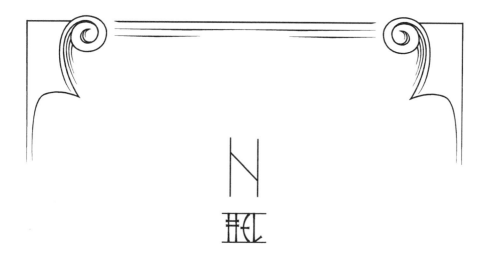

I have always thought that Hel got a bum deal. She performs a task that is both necessary and unflattering. As the goddess of the dead, she is responsible for all who die, even those who eventually go to Valhalla, and that is a heavy responsibility for any god or goddess. Unfortunately, little is known about Hel outside of her lineage, her involvement with Baldr, and Ragnarök. All three of these have been given in a dark light to showcase what can only be described as a hatchet job.

Hel is the only semi-human child of Loki. Her brothers are the wolf Fenrir and Jörmungandr the Midgard Serpent. Since Loki and her mother are both giants, Hel is really not a goddess, although she acquires the title because of her elevation as the queen of the dead in Helheim. Her description varies, but it is usually that she is dark on one side and light on the other. I have also heard her described as a rotting corpse on one side and a beautiful woman on the other. This could be metaphor, though, and in reality she could be just as beautiful as any other goddess in Asgard, and her countenance, that is, binary, could be her role as keeper of the dead: ugly and vicious at one moment to those whom she keeps, and kind and loving the next to those she sends to Valhalla.

She is also mentioned in the death of Baldr, which I mentioned in the Baldr chapter. The fact that she was willing to send Baldr back to the world of the living shows that she is not the evil malignant creature that she is often portrayed as. There are rules even for the dead and she kept to her part of the bargain. And it's not her fault that it was her father, Loki, that sent Baldr to her or kept him there. She does her job and for that she is maligned.

Much is written about her in modern literature. Heathens are quick to look for any god or goddess that seems to be attuned to their way of thinking, and with the underworld it is easy to pray to Hel for guidance and support, even though it may never come. In my novel *Three Years of Winter*, I offer up that Loki killed Baldr so that Hel could be with him in the afterlife.[37] While this is a cute piece of speculative Heathen fiction it is neither a viable nor plausible supposition. Hel does her job with precision and justice and nothing more.

Finally, Hel is often given responsibility for Ragnarök—although rumors have a way of being told in dark corners when the reality is quite different. In reality it is a combination of Loki breaking his chains and leading the dead warriors out of Helheim, Fenrir escaping his bindings, and Jörmungandr releasing his tail to escape the waters of Midgard.

And once Ragnarök is concluded, what happens next? Nowhere in the sagas does it say that Hel is killed with the other gods. Her father dies at the hands of Heimdallur. Fenrir is killed by Viðar after he kills Odin. And Jörmungandr dies by the hammer of Thor. But nothing is said about Hel. I believe she will be there at the new beginning in the hall of Náströnd to usher in the new dead and feed them to the serpent Niðhöggr.[38] There must be a queen of the dead as certainly as there are the dead.

Vert

Hel in the vert position is the queen of the dead. She is the end. While she may not represent in all cases actual and physical death, she denotes an end-

---

37. Gypsey Teague, *Three Years of Winter: Ragnarok Is No Longer a Myth* (Scott's Valley, CA: CreateSpace), 2013.

38. Seigfried, ed., *The Illustrated Völuspá*, 72, 75.

ing of significance. Take the piece seriously and look carefully at where it comes up in your spread.

Vert in the past is an ending to something, or in some cases everything. As previously stated, look carefully at where you were and what you lost. Take stock of what you have left and what you have to work with. It does you no good to accept you lost something without understanding what it was you lost and *why* you lost it in the first place. If you ignore the losses of the past you will lose them again in the future. Beware.

Vert in the present is a cautionary tale. You are possibly in the process of losing something significant. You may have already started the loss or it's coming within the foreseeable timetable, but it will arrive with or without your approval. Keep your wits about you and do whatever you can to mitigate the situation in order to lose as little as possible. However, some things *should* be lost, so look at what is at stake and what you have to gain by losing something and take that into consideration.

In the future position vert Hel gives you time to change the situation. Something you have is in danger of being lost. What it is only you may know, or you may not, but that's not Hel's problem. Look long and hard at everything you have and what is susceptible to loss or damage. If there are steps you can take to circumvent the situation, then by all means, take them. If there is nothing you can do to arrange an alternate ending to the situation, then work hard and focus all your energy on lessening the loss as best you can. Watch others during this time because often what you lose may be something someone else gains, or you may lose in a group and others may be able to assist you in avoiding the situation altogether.

Inverted

Inverted Hel is the beginning. She is rebirth and restart. That is not surprising since after Ragnarök the worlds as we know them will end but a new world will begin, and Hel will still be there doing as she does. Nothing ends that does not have a beginning to follow, even though oftentimes the new beginning is not what we anticipate or appreciate. That's the way of the worlds.

In the past inverted you started something anew. Whether it was forced upon you or you chose to begin something is irrelevant. You started something and that was enough. Take that beginning and run with it. Do the best you can, and if you were not in control to begin with, take control now. It's your life and you need to be the captain of your ship. Set the course. Raise the sails. And tack into the wind.

The present is a little different. A new beginning might be that there was a loss or ending in your past. Be of as best cheer as you can under the circumstances. Look at all the options and determine your best course of action. If the rebirth or restart is of your choosing, then you know what you are getting into. If it is of someone else's choosing, then keep both eyes open. Even though Odin gave an eye for knowledge on Mimisbrunnr, that doesn't mean that you should close one eye and hinder yourself in this. You are not Odin.

The future inverted is tricky. There are nuances to reckon with since what you do now will affect what you may lose or gain in the future. It is sometimes better to gain a little than risk it all on a lot. Do not make a fool's bet on your future. Look hard at what you have to gain and then move with confidence that you have all the information you require.

Over

Hel in the over position is deep in meaning. When Baldr came to her, she offered him a way back to the world of the living. There were decisions she had to make in order to be both fair and equitable to all sides. Did she expect every living and dead thing to ask for Baldr's release? Only Hel knows that answer, but she stuck with the decision she made and the others had to as well. The over piece are those decisions. We make them every day of our lives. Some are easy, such as what do I have for lunch, and others are mind-numbingly difficult. Whatever that decision is, you must look at all sides and be prepared for the outcome of that choice. This is Hel's position for you.

In the over past Hel is showing you that your decisions had consequences. You made them and something happened. If they were good choices then you were successful. If they were poor choices then you suffered. Either way, the decisions were made and the outcome was reached.

Hel in the over present position is presenting you with an immediate decision to make. There are no past thoughts on what you did or future plans. The decision is *now*. And the time is dire. If you take too long, the chance will pass and with it your loss or gain. Gather information but do it in a timely manner. If you hesitate or second-guess yourself then you will fail in your mission.

Future Hel over is not much better. When the decision comes, it will come without warning. Be alert to all situations and their consequences. Take nothing lightly with Hel in your over future. She will guide you as best she can, but you must be the one to determine what the choices are and which choice is the best or, in the alternative, the least negative. With knowledge comes power. And with power comes responsibility. So use your knowledge wisely or lose more than you may gain.

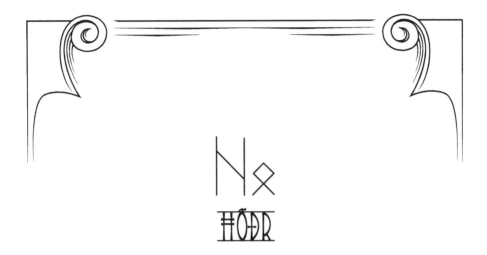

HŐÐR

Even though we may think we know much about many of the gods, we actually know very little. So few lines of text have been written down by Saxo and Snorri that we seem to create what we don't know, which can be dangerous at best and disastrous at worst. Hőðr is one of these examples. We only know two things about the god Hőðr. One is that in the Norse version he is blind and killed Baldr, possibly with the assistance, guidance, and insistence of Loki. And the second thing is that he might have been a human hero that killed Balderus and was avenged for that killing years later.

In the Snorri account of the death of Baldr, Hőðr is given a mistletoe dart by the evil trickster Loki, and through that action, Baldr dies. Shortly after that, Odin, with the giantess Rindr, creates a son, Váli. Váli's sole purpose in life is to kill Hőðr and he does, sending him to Hel.

In the second telling of the killing of Baldr, Hotherus was a human hero and not a god. He falls in love with Nanna, the daughter of King Gervaris. Unfortunately, Balderus is also in love with Nanna and they fight for her over and over until Hotherus kills Balderus. Neither marries Nanna and years later the brother of Balderus kills Hotherus in revenge.[39]

Vert

Höðr in the vert position finds the reader blind to whatever is actually happening. You see it, but you don't see it. In that I mean that you might see what is happening, but your mind's eye refuses to accept what you see, and you are blind to that which is taking place around you. It is a dangerous position to be in and one that must be corrected, if possible.

In the past the vert Höðr piece finds you suffering from something you never saw coming. It doesn't matter what that is, because whatever it is, it is serious enough to cause catastrophic changes to you and those around you. Take heed to watch yourself during this time and do everything you can to discover what caused this to happen and learn how to "see" what is going on around you. You will be safer and saner for it if you are successful.

In the present Höðr will blindside you. There is nothing you can do to mitigate the situation. You are going to be blindsided; however, it may not be a negative surprise. Many things that happen that we don't see coming may be quite pleasant: parties, birth announcements, promotions, but also some may be devastating, such as deaths, terminations, or physical suffering. To assist you in your day-to-day activities and to avoid any unexpected surprises, keep your friends and allies abreast of your situation and let them know that surprises are not something you enjoy or necessarily appreciate. Tell them, and anyone you may wish, that whatever they see coming your way you would like to know in advance. If they choose to assist you then you are in good stead. If they choose to ally with those who are there to take you by surprise then you are in the wrong crowd of friends.

Höðr in the future vert is going to shock you. It is impossible to know in the present what that shock will be, but be warned that it will happen and you won't be able to stop it. The best you may be able to do is to catch it as it is happening and therefore lessen the effect of whatever it is. That is the best-case scenario for this piece in this position.

---

39. Page, *Norse Myths*, 52.

Inverted

Inverted, the Hőðr piece leads you into something you should not be in. It's the old saying your mother probably used: If all your friends jumped off a cliff would you jump too? Here is the perfect case of that question.

In the past you were led down a wide and straight primrose path and that path turned thorny, narrow, and rocky. It's not a path you wanted to be on, but you found yourself there nonetheless. There is little that can be said for this piece in this position. Study what happened. Make changes in your situation and avoid doing this again. Even if it was safe and fun, following the crowd is never a good idea and you should caution against it in the future.

Hőðr inverted in the present gives you a look into how gullible you can be. You are in the middle of something you need not be in the middle of. It's probably a scam and one that will put you at the losing end. Get out as quickly and as safely as possible. Do not be afraid to admit you are involved, seek assistance in whatever quarter you can, and stay away from those who led you to this. Your future depends upon it.

And in the future of inverted you will be confronted with an offer that is too good to pass up. Unfortunately, it is too good and it's not true. So pass it up quickly and move along. No matter what your friends, family, or work people tell you, this is not the deal for you. There is no quick gain to riches and fame. Go back to the tried-and-true method: work for it.

Over

The over piece goes along with both the vert and inverted ones. Hőðr was trusting and gullible. He believed what Loki told him and he suffered for it, as did Baldr and even Loki, although he at least deserved it. Being gullible and easily led astray is not a trait that is sought-after. It is a dangerous trait to have, and you would be wise to get rid of it quickly.

Past Hőðr over shows where you were lost to someone else's wiles and charms. You believed the hype and trusted the person telling you. As with Hőðr and Loki, you are suffering from being too trusting, but you refuse to become jaded and cynical from the experience. Good for you. But a little distrust is not a bad thing when it is needed. You should have known that back then.

In the present this piece warns that you are in the midst of being a trusting fool. You have been approached by someone with something and you are getting ready to throw caution to the wind and jump in with both feet. Don't! Stay strong and resist the temptations of the hype and the sell. Look deeper into the facts and don't believe everything you hear or see on first contact.

Finally, the future Hőðr. If Hőðr had known then what he knew in Helheim, he would have been more cautious. He was not, but you can be. You have a trusting soul, but it's time to rein it in and take some caution. When the offer comes—and it will—look deeply into it and say no. Break the habit of being an easy mark and take back control of your life.

ᚺ

HUGINN

Odin is known by a number of symbols and artifacts. Two of those are his ravens that sit on his high seat of Hliðskjálf when he is in Asgard, or on his shoulders when he is out in the world. Huginn and Muninn are these two ravens. Huginn is Thought and Muninn is Memory. Together they keep the All Father appraised of the goings on in Midgard daily.

When Odin gave speech to his two ravens, he in essence created spies for all the ages. Each morning he sends them out into the world and each night he worries that something will keep them from returning, although they always do.

Thought is an interesting concept. It is a higher brain function and one that takes cognition. The ravens may be that wise, since ravens are smart birds and may be trained to do all sorts of tricks, but they are tricks and they are trained. To say that a raven has thought is prosopopoeial. However, Odin's ravens may be able to speak. They might even be highly intelligent. In the end, does it really matter? If they report what they see, then they are only recorders. And that's all they need to be.

Vert

Huginn has clear vision. The eyes of a raven are sharp and able to see far distances. In Huginn's instance not only does he see but he reports. Therefore, he is a type of reporter, giving Odin the nightly news every evening. Without this the All Father would have to venture forth himself and even though he is a god, and a mighty one at that, he is only one god and there is a lot of ground to cover in the nine realms.

In the past, Huginn is your clear vision. You can see everything that is going on and you can parse it. When you needed information, you received it and you were pleased with the results. It was Huginn who enabled you to win in these situations, and because of that, be thankful and grateful—not always the same thing. Also look at what you learned and what you saw and put that to good use.

The present Huginn piece in vert is where you need to be to see everything necessary. Your eyes are not always open, and they need to be in this situation. A lot of things are happening at the same time, and without the knowledge of Huginn you may lose some of that to the din of extraneous information. However, be advised that what you see is not always what you should believe, and what you believe is not always what you want it to be.

Future Huginn will extend your vision well into the future. You will have the power to see through others' obfuscation. No lie or falsehood will get past you and you will know the difference between truth and untruth. Do not throw this knowledge in anyone's face, though, for that shows contempt of others' abilities, and you will need these others soon enough. Be humble in your vision and others will admire you for it.

Inverted

Inverted Huginn is confusion. Even though Odin sends him out every day to see what is out there, things may become confused at times. If you tell enough people the same story, eventually the story becomes muddled and loses its accuracy. This is Huginn inverted. No matter what you see, you still cannot make heads or tails of it.

Past inverted Huginn was your loss of clarity. You were in a fog for a long time and nothing has made any sense. However, in the present you are now able to look to the past and see what was invisible to you then. Even though it may be too late to apply the information you had then, you at least have the knowledge now. Use it to repair what was broken and avoid what is still to come.

In the present the confusion is everywhere. Nothing you do makes sense. Whatever anyone tells you goes in one ear and out the other. There is little clarity, and everything is lost to the crowd. Even though that is going on all around you, there is still a chance to rectify this situation by applying concentration to the problem and parsing out what you can see versus what you can't. Eventually, with hard work and diligence, you can cut through the fog and determine what is necessary to complete the puzzle. It may take you well into the future, but it can be done if you believe in yourself and your surroundings.

Speaking of the future, Huginn inverted will allow you to confuse others through your wit and charm. You have perfect sight around you, but with your words and deeds you will cast clouds about others, causing them to lose sight of the prize, the problem, or the situation. This can be used to your advantage in business, romance, or travel. Be certain to think through your conversation before beginning it and know your audience. Just because you have Huginn in your future does not mean that someone else doesn't also. And when two Huginns conflict with each other in the future, only one may be victorious.

Over

Seeing and observing are two different things. So, too, are information and knowledge. Observing is knowledgeable seeing, and knowledge is processed information with the addition of practice. All that means is just because you see does not mean you know, and just because you have information does not mean you can use it. Huginn in the future is the culmination of both seeing and information. You now have the ability to observe and know. Use it wisely. It is not an ability that is gained by many.

The past over finds you knowing too much. You have observed everything around you and applied what you observed to what you knew. Your world is now tainted by what you have experienced, and you cannot undo that. There is a saying that "I can't unsee that." This is the application here in the past. What you have witnessed is indelibly inked in your brain and you are stuck with it. Make the most of it and learn from it. And remember, whatever you know now will be priceless soon.

In the present you are the "smart one." You know all the answers because you can collect what you observe and apply that information to the present issues at hand. Others will come to you for assistance and you will gladly give it to them. Some may resent that you have all the answers, but you cannot do anything about that in the present. You are on a path of assistance and whatever you do is written down and cannot be altered.

It's the future that you will pay for what you knew and what you observed in the past. You saw too much and did not keep it to yourself. Now you must repair those bridges without burning new ones. People you trusted were not what they appeared to be, and you failed to see that. You didn't know that you needed to be careful around others and now everyone that had an agenda is out for you and you will have to work extra hard to keep from falling victim to your well-meaning. You are able to in the long run, but it will take a long time and you may feel that you are going to fall short before it is over. You won't, so don't give up hope. Drive forward and stay the course. All will be resolved eventually.

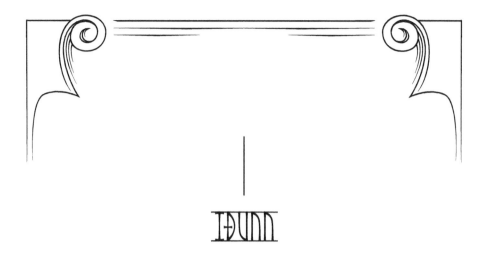

IÐUNN

Iðunn is probably the most important goddess in the entire pantheon. Without her there would be no magical fruit to keep the gods and goddesses young and vibrant. And when she was kidnapped and her fruit was kept from the gods, they were sorely at a loss for them. As the wife of Bragi she is a citizen of Asgard and, as such, a member of the Æsir.

I specifically say *fruit* because it is unlikely that Iðunn had apples. The apple was not introduced to Scandinavia until well after the Norse countries converted to Christianity. It is more likely that the word used to denote the apple was a word that meant any fruit or product from a tree, such as a nut. Snorri most likely used the word *apple* since it was of Christian origin and was more understandable to his reading audience.

That notwithstanding, the meaning is clear that without the magic fruit the immortality of the gods would end and so would they. In the kidnapping story, Loki is tricked into exchanging his safety for the magic fruit of Iðunn. While he, Hoenir, and Odin were out exploring they slaughtered an ox for dinner. It would not cook until an eagle came by and offered to lift the spell of rawness from the meat in exchange for the best cuts. After they agreed, the meat was cooked and the eagle feasted.

Loki took exception to this and struck at the eagle with a large stick. The eagle flew up high in the air with the stick in its talons and Loki still holding on. Loki promised anything if the eagle would take him safely back to the ground and the deal was the fruit of Iðunn. Once back in Asgard, Loki tricked Iðunn to go with him and the eagle, who was actually the giant Þjazi, captured her.

As the gods aged, Loki finally told the truth of what had happened, and Odin said if Loki could not return Iðunn and her magical fruit then Odin would kill Loki. Using Freyja's falcon cloak, Loki flew to Jotunheim, brought Iðunn back with him, and in the process Þjazi, again in the form of the eagle, was killed. Once the fruits were distributed to the citizens of Asgard, all was right with the realm.

Vert

Iðunn in the vert position is immortality. You will live forever—well, at least your name or fame will. No one lives forever, not even the gods. Thanks to the fruits of Iðunn, time passes slowly and, with it, the world around us.

In the past the vert piece shows you looking for the fame and name recognition you feel you so richly deserve. It may not be warranted, but at that moment in the past you didn't care. You did what it took to gain that greatness and you were willing to do anything to keep it. Look to what it cost you and how it will impact your present and future.

In the present the vert piece of Iðunn is one of longing and want. You know what you want and what you need to do to get it. However, there are many players out there that are in your way. Look and ask if immortality at any cost is worth it. Do you want to be known internationally no matter how or what you do, or do you want to be known locally for something worthwhile? It's a question that you will have to answer before you may move forward.

The future vert finds you contemplating what it is you really want. Is it fame and fortune that will last forever? Is it notoriety? Are you a sinner or a saint? It's important to ascertain this before starting this path.

Inverted

Inverted, the Iðunn piece is sickness and death. This is not the death of an idea or a stage just to start another one. This is *death*! Without the magic fruit there is no life, and the inverted Iðunn takes all that from you. There is pestilence. There is suffering. And yes, there is death.

The past inverted is where you lost much. Your sickness might have been physical, mental, or spiritual. There is death around you, but then, there is death around all of us. However, this death is close, and you have felt it more severely than anything else you have known. That you made it through is a testament to your willpower and spirit. Take consolation that you made it and you have your life in front of you.

The present inverted is a place of misery and woe. Your sickness and death, either actual or metaphoric, is all around you. Seek solace from those you trust and take their suggestions to heart. They are your friends and your allies, and they will help you get through this period. Although you are strong enough to make it on your own, it is safer and easier to take this journey with others—especially if they have also walked the same path as where you are now.

Future inverted Iðunn is a warning of what will come. Take this seriously. Your health and your well-being are in jeopardy, and without planning you will suffer extensively. Guard your health. Watch your back. Take no risks or chances that may come back to haunt you, for this is not the time to be complacent about any of that. Your life is in danger. Use this knowledge well.

Over

Iðunn over is her health and caring role. She is the one responsible for keeping the gods alive and she takes that chore seriously. Without her there would be no Asgard. Ragnarök would have already started and the gods would be old and dead long before their time.

Iðunn in the past puts you in the roll of caregiver. Whether it was your children or your parents, you were there when they needed you and you kept them as well as possible for as long as you could. Take comfort in the fact that you did a good job and you are worthy. It is not an easy chore to watch over people and care for them in their most vulnerable times.

In the present Iðunn finds you contemplating being a caregiver to another. This position is not the same as the past, although it is easy to fall into that mindset. Look long and hard before you agree to be that assistant. Even though this may be your family you are being asked to help, there are other agencies that might do a better job. Be the facilitator in this case.

The future Iðunn is a warning. If you are not more careful with your own health, it will be yourself that you will be concerned with. Diet, exercise, stress, all the things that affect your well-being. Take stock of your life and make changes *now*. Remember what I said about Iðunn being death. It's one thing to have death all around you. It's another thing to have death knocking at your door and you are the one being asked to go.

JÖRMUNGANDR

Jörmungandr is the offspring of Loki and the giantess Angrboða. When he was born, Odin took the great serpent and exiled it to the seas around Midgard. As the serpent grew, it encircled the entire world and grasped its own tail. It is also called the Midgard Serpent, and when it releases its tail it will be one of the conditions of Ragnarök.

At Ragnarök, Jörmungandr and Thor will fight until they both die. This will not be the first time the two will meet but it will be the last one. The first time the two met was at the castle of Útgarða-Loki, not to be confused with Loki the companion of Thor. Útgarða-Loki is the chief of the castle Útgarða in Jotunheim.

While visiting the castle, Thor was challenged to pick up a cat. Try as he might, he could only pick one paw off the ground. Each time he tried, the cat would arch its back, and even though Thor was able to get the cat to almost the ceiling, the paws and tail were still touching the ground. The next day as Thor was leaving the castle, Útgarða-Loki told Thor that if he had known of the god's strength he would never have let him in and he never would again.

The cat that Thor was attempting to lift was actually Jörmungandr, the Midgard Serpent. And Útgarða-Loki was terrified that Thor might pick it up and disrupt the entire universe by separating the serpent from its tail.

The next time Thor met Jörmungandr is when the god of thunder went fishing for him. With the giant Hymir in the boat, Thor went fishing for the Midgard Serpent. Using an ox head, Thor threw out his line and the serpent took the bait. While wrestling with the serpent, Thor's feet went through the bottom of the boat and threatened to sink both the god and the giant. In a feat of desperation, Hymir cut the line that was hooked to the serpent and Jörmungandr swam away.

I find this story difficult to accept for one glaring reason: Jörmungandr is biting his own tail. He is to keep his tail until he releases it at Ragnarök. If Jörmungandr took the bait, then he would have had to release his tail to do so. That would have ushered in the end of the worlds. But when Thor is separated from the serpent, the world stays just where it is.

Vert

Jörmungandr vert is the status quo. As long as the great serpent keeps its tail in its mouth, the world will go on as it should. Only by releasing the tail would Ragnarök ensue. Balance in all things comes with the Jörmungandr piece in vert.

In the past the vert Jörmungandr has your life in perfect harmony. There is neither strife nor grief. All is as it should be. Even though you may think that the world around you is in chaos, you are actually in balance with your surroundings. Many things have had a go at you and many times you have been set upon, but you have always survived and regained your control and composure. Bring this into the present and you will continue your harmony with your surroundings.

In the present, balance is out of kilter. You are not in danger of spinning out of control, but there are forces against you that threaten your harmony. Pay close attention to those around you and look at what they are doing to curtail what you are doing. Like Hymir, some may be cutting ropes to dislodge your confidence or success. Like the cat, there may be things that are concealed, and they are the things that are at the center of your issues. Whatever "they" are, you must seek them out, correct them, and set your balance aright.

In the future the Jörmungandr piece is lost balance. You had balance and control for a long time. Now something will threaten that. There are no maps or guides to help you find your way in this. You will have to seek your own path and mark your own trail. In the end, though, all will be right again, and you will prevail. Stay the course and believe in yourself. As the mighty Thor trusted Mjölnir, trust those around you and, especially, trust yourself. Your internal compass guides true. Use it.

Inverted

Jörmungandr holds fast to his tail as Fafnir held to his gold. It is the one constant in his world, and until he releases it at Ragnarök he is secure in that sensation. In the inverted position this steadfastness and stubbornness is a constant that is all around you. To emulate Jörmungandr in this position is to invite disaster, but the known is oftentimes better than the unknown and even though the great serpent holds fast his tail, he shall do so because it is all he knows.

In the past the Jörmungandr piece is exactly what you would expect: a refusal to let go. You have held on to things too long and it's time to release your grip and let them slide away. Unlike Jörmungandr, Ragnarök would not have descended upon you with this action, but like the great serpent, you refused to believe that. You held to a belief or an item so steadfastly that you lost all sight of everything else. Beware of this and look to your present to change your behavior. It did you no good and has done you great harm.

In the present the Jörmungandr piece is one of collecting. Unlike the past where you were holding firmly with little reason to, in the present you are holding onto something for a reason and you know what that reason is. *And it is forcing you to change your behavior to accommodate that collection.* Individuals who often see Jörmungandr in their present are referred to as hoarders. They collect incessantly and without control. You have that possibility if you are not careful.

The future is just one day away. The Jörmungandr piece warns you to take it slow and easy, everything in moderation. It is fine to collect things. It is all well and good to want to keep the familiar around you. But do not dwell on having too much and keeping it for too long. Practice catch and release. If it is important to you, then use it, but then pass it on to someone else. Practice minimalism. It keeps you from overburdening yourself with possessions. Let them go.

Over

Jörmungandr is destruction beyond comprehension. Once he is released at Ragnarök he will destroy everything in his path until Thor confronts him and they die nine steps apart. Even before the great serpent releases his tail, the catastrophe is imminent. Jörmungandr is disaster waiting to happen. And there is nothing we can do to curtail that destruction.

In the past your Jörmungandr piece in over was the avoidance of the destruction and chaos that the serpent is capable of. You have dodged danger on many occasions to the amazement of many. Your luck seems to have no end and you are able to sidestep any disaster. Unfortunately, this streak cannot last forever, and even though you have had great success in your past, it is about to come to a screeching end. Prepare for the luck to run out.

Over in the present is where you pay the price. Dire consequences are all about you and your life is about to change significantly, even more than it already has, and you feel that it's bad now. Your world is being beset by one problem after another and there seems to be no relief for that. Oftentimes our complex world that we try to make easier with electronics and machines only succeeds in cluttering up the world we are seeking. These clutterings have come home to roost and with them they have brought problems beyond number. The only solution to this is to ride the storm as best you can and look for the relief that is coming.

Jörmungandr over in the future is the best outcome you can hope for. You have had your share of problems, both serious and annoying. Now is the time to rid yourself of these and smite them. However, do not emulate Thor at Ragnarök. Do not become fixated on the problem to the extent that you forsake all other issues. That will be your demise, either actual or metaphoric.

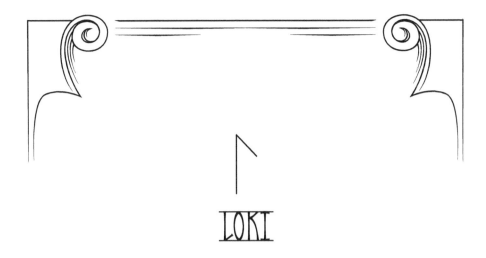

LOKI

Loki, unlike his daughter Hel, has gotten a better reception in modern times. His role in Heathenry has turned from one of disgust to one of admiration, and with the latest series of movies out, one of outright lust. Loki, though, warrants none of this positive attention. He is the chaos to the universe, and similar to Coyote in the Native American traditions, he moves in a circle of his own making and choosing, calling out that which he sees fit and enjoying the disharmony of the gods for his own amusement.

Loki is married to Sigyn and they have two children: Nari (who is also referred to as Narfi) and Vali, who are both killed by Odin when he is captured after the death of Baldr. He has three children by Angrboða: Hel, Fenrir, and Jörmungandr. Fenrir is imprisoned in Asgard and Jörmungandr is tail-tied around Midgard. Hel is Queen of Helheim and at least has her own realm to rule over. Loki is also the mother of Sleipnir by the steed Svaðilfari.

Even though he is given the title of god by many, he is not one. He is a giant, a Jotun, and one from the cold realm of Svartalfheim. He is significant in the sagas from the beginning of the building of the wall around Asgard to the end of times with Ragnarök.

As Asgard was being created, the gods knew they could not survive attacks by other races. To that end, they determined to build a wall around the realm to protect it. One day a builder came to the gods and offered to build a wall. His payment was Freyja, the sun, and the moon. His offer was without merit, but Loki convinced the gods to accept the offer on certain conditions. Those were that he concluded his work in one season and that no man may assist him.

The builder agreed, with the counteroffer that he be allowed to use his steed Svaðilfari. The gods saw no problem with that, and the builder began his work. From the beginning it was clear that the steed was no ordinary horse since it could do twice or thrice the work that any other horse could do. The wall went up quicker than was expected and it looked as though the wall would be completed prior to the allotted time.

The gods set upon Loki for convincing them to accept this offer and Odin said that if the wall was completed before the time limit, Odin would kill Loki. To save his life, Loki turned himself into a beautiful mare and lured the steed away from the builder. As this was the builder's only "ace in the hole," he was unable to complete the work in time. At this point Odin realized that the builder was a Jotun, although why he couldn't recognize a frost giant before or why Loki didn't alert the All Father of such a disguise is never explained. Odin had Thor kill the builder. When Loki returned as the mare, he'd had a foal with the steed. The foal was grey and had eight legs. It was named Sleipnir and presented to Odin to carry the All Father into battles and across the great realms. This is probably the only time when Loki had to suffer for his folly and his chaos, with the exception of the death of Baldr, which is in an entirely different level of pain and suffering.

In other chapters we have discussed the loss of Sif's hair, the kidnapping of Iðunn, and theft of Mjölnir. We touched upon the part Loki had in the death of Baldr, but not to the degree that shows how he ended up chained to a rock until Ragnarök.

When Odin realized that Baldr was dead indirectly at the hand of Loki, he sought out the trickster. Loki was no fool; he knew he was in danger and fled to the mountains. There he built a house with doors open to all four sides so he could see who was coming and to give him a way out. As the gods approached, Loki transformed into a salmon and swam away. The gods tried to capture the trickster with their net, but Loki first went under it and then, after the gods added weights to the net, he tried to jump over it. Thor caught Loki and they took him back to Asgard where they chained him to a great stone using the entrails of his son Narfi. Above him Skadi placed a serpent to drip venom on Loki day and night. Loki's wife, Sigyn, sits next to her husband with a bowl to catch the venom. When she must empty it, the venom strikes Loki, causing the trickster so much pain that he writhes against the stones and earthquakes shake all of Asgard and Midgard.[40] He will stay imprisoned until the final day at Ragnarök.

Vert

Loki vert is one of deceit and trickery. Loki cannot be trusted. Even when he is doing something for someone else it is usually because he was forced to or to correct something he did to someone. The Loki vert piece shows a great deal of behind-the-scenes chicanery and scheming. Nothing is what it seems, and even if you see it you should not believe it.

In the past a Loki vert piece gives you the place of having been deceived. You were lied to. You were conned. You were taken advantage of. And there was nothing you could do to stop it or abate the situation. Whatever it was, it was serious, and it must be remembered but it cannot be dwelled upon. Move on with your life and be more careful in the future. Even if you have the chance to seek or achieve revenge, do not take it. Nothing good will come of stooping to the level of Loki.

In the present there is mischief around you. You may not see it yet, but it will happen. Be aware of that and cautious of the situation. Loki is not only a trickster but a changeling. People are not who or what they say they are. Double- or triple-check everything before you make a decision. It will behoove you to be extraordinarily careful during this time.

In the future Loki vert piece, you are the one who is the deceiver. There is something that you will need to accomplish and you feel you need to be less than honest or true in order to finalize this act. While the path looks straight and wide, it is fraught with peril. Do not reduce yourself to that level. Be as

---

40. Seigfried, ed., *The Illustrated Völuspá*, 67.

Heimdallur: honorable and self-sacrificing. Emulating Loki will only put you at his level, and once you reduce yourself to that, you will be tied to him forever.

Inverted

Inverted the Loki piece is selfishness. Loki was in it for himself. There was no humanitarian motivation in anything he did. As I said earlier, anything he did that was positive was because he was trying to save his own neck, which he had to do literally once when he lost a bet. Too many are currently emulating the trickster in this regard. They only think of themselves and the rest of the realms can suffer.

Inverted past reminds you that you and those around you have suffered the selfishness of the trickster. You have done things that you should not have and hurt people that didn't deserve it. You will be punished for these transgressions, so be prepared for that. The piece in this position merely reminds you that whatever you do has consequences, and even if you evaded them today, there is always tomorrow, and eventually you will face Hel and she knows everything about you and will judge you accordingly.

Present inverted is the selflessness piece. It is the opposite of the past. You are the humanitarian who will do anything for anyone. There is a price to pay, though, for this and if you are not careful you will be called to pay it sooner than you planned. That does not mean you should forego your humanitarianism; it merely means you need to balance your actions with your consequences.

In the future the inverted Loki warns you that you are capable of great things, but at a great price. Do not become Fafnir. A man who hoards is not a man; he is a beast with only one thought—that of acquiring more. Temper your actions with wisdom and slay the desire to keep everything for yourself.

Over

When the Loki piece is pulled over, you are being forced to be helpful. There is no choice in the matter. Whatever you did to put yourself in this situation is serious enough to have to get out of it. And on the flip side of this coin, whatever you see that needs assistance, you will do whatever it takes to be of assistance.

Past Loki over gives you a sense of worth. You have done great things for others, but you didn't do it out of altruism. There was a force behind you pushing, yes, literally, pushing you to do it. Take no malice from this. For whatever reason you did the good deed, you paid the price and the karma that will come of it is worth what you paid. If you were paying a debt you owed, then accept the debt. If you were seduced into being kind and helpful, then accept that also. Acceptance to this assistance is the key here.

Present over finds you contemplating forcing another to help you. If you need help, then ask. If someone does not wish to assist you, then ask another. Forcing someone to do anything, even if it is something helpful, will only make them angry and distant. Nothing good comes from force. You push, they push harder. Then you push again and they push harder or get others to push with them. Eventually you have entire groups in conflict.

In the future with the Loki over piece you have the choice. You may either accept being forced to help or you may choose not to. I know that sounds odd, but it makes sense in the long run. Oftentimes we are "asked" for help when we don't wish to. Your friend asks for a ride and you would rather stay home. He is your friend, so you feel obligated to help him. But you don't want to. However, you do anyway because he is your friend. You are forced by friendship to assist him. You are going to be in a similar situation soon. Look hard and deep at the reason for the request and who is making it. In the end, if you choose not to help, do not let yourself be manipulated. Stand your ground and make your choice. Then take whatever fallout comes from it.

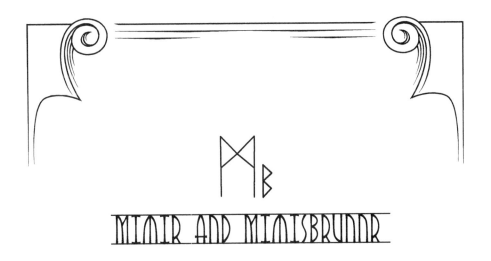

MIMIR AND MIMISBRUNNR

Mimisbrunnr is the stream or well of Mimir. Since the two are inseparable after the Æsir-Vanir war, it makes sense to discuss both as one. Mimir was a giant and Odin's uncle since he was the brother of Bestla, the wife of Bor and the mother of Odin, Vili, and Ve. He was a great scholar and when the Vanir requested hostages after the war with the Æsir, they got Hoenir and Mimir. As we described earlier, Hoenir was the less-knowledgeable one, and after discovering that Mimir was the wisest one, they felt betrayed by the Æsir. Why they didn't cut Hoenir's head off I could never figure out, but instead they beheaded Mimir and sent his head back to Odin, who stuffed it and kept it viable with magic and herbs.

Before the war, though, when the head and body were still attached, Mimir guarded one of the three streams that fed Yggdrasil: the one from Jotunheim. Odin came to Mimir one day and asked for a drink of the waters so that he might gain wisdom and knowledge as Mimir had done. Mimir, knowing that knowledge requires sacrifice, told the All Father that he must sacrifice one of his eyes to gain the sight of the waters. Odin plucked out his eye and presented it to Mimir and thus drank of the waters. With that drink, Odin gained his knowledge.

Vert

Mimir was blamed for the failure of Hoenir, and in the vert position others blame you as well. It doesn't matter whether it's your fault or not; whatever is wrong, you will get the blame. Whether you lose your head over it or not is speculative, but the bottom line is that the betrayal that you will feel at being left out to dry is significant.

In the past position the vert piece is where you blamed someone else for your failure. It isn't an honorable thing to do, but you did it anyway and got away with it, at least for the moment. Watch your back, though, because no secret stays a secret forever. Those who took the blame will be back, and they will be ever more able to show the world it was your fault than you will be able to avoid it. Remember, you have been warned.

The present is where you are about to get the blame and punishment for something you had nothing to do with. Your business and personal affairs are not what you think they are, and there are people behind the scenes working hard to make you the scapegoat in this situation. There is little you can do at the moment to allay others' suspicions, so bide your time, keep your head high (no pun intended), and wait your time to have your day. You will eventually be found to be the innocent party in this, and the guilty ones will be punished.

The future finds you in a sticky situation. You know that someone else is about to get blamed for something they didn't do, and you can protect them if you speak up. However, you also have had dealings with the individual who is about to be blamed and you want revenge even if it's not by your direct hand. Here is where you must take the moral high ground, for if you don't, then you won't be able to look anyone in the eyes again. Even though this person has wronged you, you must speak up to clear them. Unfortunately, the person you clear will still be against you, but at least you will have known that you did the right thing and others will too. There is power in honor. This time the power is on your side.

Inverted

Mimir at his well kept great knowledge and secrets that most would never know. For a price, he was willing to share these, and that price was severe. Even though Odin gained great wisdom through the waters of the well, it took even greater strength to pluck his own eye out in order to pass it over to Mimir. Could any of us do that? *Would* any of us do that is a better question, I think. The inverted piece is such a situation. There is wisdom but it will come at a price, and the price may be higher than anyone is willing to pay.

The past finds you willing to do anything for information and knowledge. You are a student of the world and you want it all. No price is too high to pay and you have done some things that cost you dearly in your pursuit. Reconcile these experiences as what you gained and balance them out. Did you get a good return on your investment? Was the price worth the product? Are you still paying? If the answer is yes, then work very hard to get your balance sheet evened out. It does no one any good to go into the future owing or being in debt. And you know that, don't you?

The present inverted piece is one of great secrets that you have and others want. Secrets, as I said before, are never secrets forever. The best thing to do with them is never acquire them in the first place, but now you have them and you're stuck with them. Rid yourself of them as quickly as possible. If they are dangerous to let out, then bury them deep and let others reveal them. If they are simple truths that would hurt or humiliate others, then temper them and release them. Whatever you do, *do not* keep them secret. They will only harm you more than those they concern.

In the future you are going to have a quest. That quest will be in the classical sense and it will involve exploration and adventure. The object of this quest will be the answers that have haunted you all your life. Only you know what those are and only you will know if you have achieved your objective. Whether you do or you do not is not the issue. The important thing is the quest itself. You will learn as you go and it will make you a better person, and through that quest you will gain the wisdom and knowledge that not even Mimisbrunnr could provide.

Over

After Mimir's head was separated from his body, his head was kept alive by Odin using magic. And thanks to that magic Mimir will continue to offer Odin wise council right up until Ragnarök. The words of Mimir resonated with the All Father and Odin was able to do great things with the knowledge that he gained at the well and through his uncle Mimir. The over position of this piece is such council. Wisdom is not truly understood until it is applied. This is where the application happens.

Past over there was great wisdom, but it was ill-used. Knowledge is not only for the altruistic. Knowledge is a commodity that is available to anyone. If you have enough information and you have enough time to process that information, then you can produce knowledge. It's not magic. It's application. And in the past there was great knowledge that was used for less-than-honorable objectives. You were involved at some point in this, and you are now trying to extricate yourself from that situation. The past issues have followed you into the present, and if you do not remove yourself from the situation, then it shall follow you into the future. Do whatever it takes to get away from this ordeal; remember how you ended up in the situation and avoid doing it again.

Present over is wisdom in general. Everyone is wise around you and everyone wants to help everyone else. Enjoy the moment. Don't overthink this and go with the flow. No one is out to get you, and everyone is what they appear to be.

In the future, though, it is dark and gloomy. If you are not careful in your present, then the future will hold a loss of wisdom and that will put you in a dire predicament. Secrets are never secret for long and some secrets, especially those that are proprietary, contain wisdom not meant for everyone. It's a wise person who knows when to shut up and sit down. Whether you are the one with or without the secrets is still up for grabs, but either way it will behoove you to look closely at what you tell whom and when.

MISTLETOE

Mistletoe itself is a semiparasitic plant that draws both food and water from the host tree. Interesting also is that the plant is toxic to small children, animals, and older persons. So even though the plant seldom kills the host tree or plant, it can kill those who ingest it. I believe this is where the tragedy of mistletoe comes from in the death of Baldr. The Norse knew of the simple mistletoe and how it affected those who took it as a medicine as well as how it affected the hosts. It was a short jump to use it as the insignificant plant to kill a god with.

In the death of Baldr, as we spoke of in the Baldr chapter, Frigg secured an oath from every living and dead thing, person or not, in the nine realms to do no harm to her son Baldr. However, the mistletoe was such an insignificant plant that Frigg, even in all her wisdom, thought that the plant was harmless. This is the secret of the mistletoe. It is neither insignificant nor harmless.

Vert

Mistletoe in the vert position is one of great insignificance. It is not to be said that the plant is insignificant, but that those who look upon it see insignificance. If Frigg had thought of the plant as a worthy growth, then Baldr might still be alive. However, she and everyone else thought of the lowly mistletoe as a parasite. A pariah. And nothing that warranted attention. As I said above, mistletoe is neither insignificant nor harmless. Do not be fooled by those whom you think are below you. You could be dismissive of mistletoe.

Vert in the past is you. You are the mistletoe. You have been looked over, dismissed, ignored. For whatever reason—and it may be because of your own actions or the actions of others, or even the blindness of those who do not see—you have been cast aside and forgotten. Whatever the situation, you must not take it seriously or personally. That will only make matters worse and you will be like the mistletoe in the saga. You will be labelled as the reason for all the negativity that has happened around you.

It is important to take the high ground. Even though the action has happened and you are now feeling the full weight of what has occurred, take the time to validate yourself to those around you without resorting to negative behavior. And whatever you do, do not become a vehicle for someone else's action. There are many Lokis out in the world and it only takes one Höðr to ruin everything. Don't fall into being used by Loki or becoming Höðr.

In the present the vert mistletoe is you looking down or askance at someone else. I know it's easy to do in this day and age, to relegate someone to a lesser status. I learned a long time ago humanity must always have "the other" to blame. The problem with that is it not only insults the individual or group that is being dismissed, but it casts great shame on the one dismissing.

Instead, take the time to understand the situation of the other person or group. Study their case and look through their eyes and walk with their feet. You will find that they are not any different from you once you put aside your prejudices and opinions. Further, if they have been dismissed or ignored for a long period of time, it may take more than a moment or an hour or a day to gain their trust. As with the giants and the Æsir, we are all more similar than different.

The future vert mistletoe is a mix of the past and the present. There is going to be a situation where someone or a group will be dismissed and ignored for who or what they are. It may be your group or yourself, or it may be another group or individual. Either way, the course of action is the same. You must meet each other halfway. It only takes one gnome—and I don't mean the cute garden gnomes that populate your backyard, I mean the general truth and aphorism applied to an idea—to see that we are not that separated.

Inverted

The inverted mistletoe is being taken advantage of against your will. As Höðr was used as a vehicle to murder by Loki, so too may you be used to do very bad or very good things. Either way, it is against your will and is wrong. You have the right to do as you wish and not be manipulated by another.

In the past the inverted mistletoe warns that you were used and didn't know it. Look hard now to see what happened and how to either abate the damage in the present or avoid such damage in the future. As with all other actions, take no overt retaliation to those who did you wrong. Never stoop to their level; just avoid them in the future and avoid putting yourself in the same situation. Remember, forewarned is forearmed and this is one of the best examples.

In the present there are situations where many may be abused either mentally or physically by others and you have the potential to remedy the situation. Tread carefully, though, because powerful entities are at work behind the scenes, and if you fall on the wrong side of these it will be you that will be part of the group being abused.

You are a wise and careful individual. You have the tool set to repair the damages that are being created without actual involvement. You just have to think about what you need to do and what you need to say at the proper time to rectify the situation. Be like Bragi with his silver tongue. Use your wiles to sway the situation to your benefit and the benefit of those who are afflicted. You can do it. You just need to believe in yourself.

The future mistletoe inverted is nothing like anything else you will find. This is the beginning of death and destruction. The dart was a metaphor for the evil in the world and it's coming to take advantage of everyone and everything. If you find this piece in your future, know that nothing good will come from it.

Over

Prepare for the worst and hope for the best. Pull your family and your friends that you trust close to you and anchor your boats to the shore. Storms will rise and darkness will cover you, but if you are prepared it will blow over quickly and you will come through unscathed. Do not take this lightly. There is great damage to be done to you and yours if you allow it. Don't allow it!

In the past, you and yours have had your share of calamity. It has passed but there are lingering segments still clinging to you that you must not bring into the present. As you look back on what you had and what you may still be afflicted with, you must deal with it soon since it will do you no good if you ignore it. Be vigilant now. Do not tarry thinking that you can wait and all will clear up. It doesn't work that way with the over mistletoe.

Now, in the present, is the time to look around you for what may be threatening the beauty of your home and hearth. Danger lurks in the shadows and it won't take much to bring it out to kill all that you have worked for. Do not be paranoid, though. The cautious mind is one that is open and always thinking. The closed mind is a trap for everything. Be like the cautious mind and look about you for the clues to stay the progress of the death.

Future mistletoe will happen before you even realize it. The death of everything you love will happen with or without your knowledge or consent. The best you can do is collect those items and people that will help you put yourself back together again after the destruction passes. Nature does not lend itself to leash, and unlike Fenrir with Gleipnir, nature cannot be tricked into thinking it's a game or a puzzle. Nature does what nature wants to do. The best we can do is pick up the pieces.

MJÖLNIR

Mjölnir is the hammer of Thor. When Loki cut the golden tresses of Sif, he was sent to the dwarves of Svartalfheim to request the dwarves, the sons of Ivaldi, to make new golden hair for the goddess. As they did it, they also made two other grand items: Skidbladnir and Gungnir. (Skidbladnir was the fantastic ship that could be folded up and put away in a cloak pocket. Gungnir was the spear of Odin that never missed its intended target.) After these items were completed, Loki approached two other dwarves, the brothers Brokkr and Sindri, and challenged them to create three greater gifts for the gods, greater than the sons of Ivaldi made. In the wager Loki bet his head that they would not best the other dwarves.

Brokkr and Sindri first made Gullinbursti, which was given to Freyjr as a gift. The magical boar had hairs that glowed golden in the dark. They then created the magic ring Draupnir. This ring could and did duplicate itself every ninth night with eight duplicate rings. As the brothers were forging these items Loki, in the guise of a fly, would create havoc with Brokkr as he pumped the bellows, but the steadfast dwarf kept the fires hot and Sindri completed the two tasks.

However, when the brothers began to create a magic hammer for the god of thunder, Loki saw that he might lose the bet, so he intensified his aggravation of Brokkr. The two instances before, Loki as a fly drew blood from the body of Brokkr, but this time Loki stung the dwarf in the eye and the blood from his eye caused the dwarf to stop momentarily to wipe the blood away, which was enough to cause the handle of the hammer to be shorter than was intended. This, though, was not enough to hinder the power of the hammer and the dwarves all went to Asgard to present their gifts.

When Odin received these, the brothers Brokkr and Sindri had the greatest gifts and attempted to claim Loki's head. The trickster, though, said that in order to take his head they would have to damage his neck and that was not part of the bargain. Unable to claim Loki's head, the brothers sewed Loki's mouth shut and left.

Mjölnir is a powerful weapon used to destroy those who threaten Asgard and the gods within. Thor is seldom seen without it and when he loses it, which happens from time to time, he is bereft without it and must seek assistance, usually from Loki, to regain it.

Vert

In the vert position the piece of Mjölnir is power unmatched. With his gloves and belt and wielding Mjölnir, Thor is able to defeat any and all enemies of Asgard, and he is quick to use it for that purpose. Power, though, without direction or intelligence behind it is just power. There is no finesse to it and no guidance. These are important things to remember when dealing with Mjölnir.

In the past Mjölnir was you: unbridled power. It has gotten you into trouble and you have had to work hard to get out of those situations. Unlike Thor killing giants, you are not Thor and power without guidance has proven a dangerous friend to you. You will be wise to learn from your mistake and trust the guidance given to you by others and by your own counsel when next you bring out the "big hammer."

In the present position Mjölnir gives you the chance to show how much power you have and what you can do with it. This is the perfect time to show off and be the hero in the situation, but that is a fallacy. All this situation is going to do is show others that you don't have the maturity and self-control to have the power you have either taken or been given.

It is imperative that you wait this out and do nothing rash or foolish. In the end you can still be the hero, but it may take more patience and control than you feel you have at the moment. You do have that control and patience; you just have to believe in yourself and eventually all things will come to you.

The future vert is a chance to give the power away to another who needs it more than you do. You were in this situation before, and you were given this power by one who had it in order to assist someone close to you. Now it's your turn to pass that power on, and it will be greatly appreciated when it is given.

Ask for nothing in return. Do not think of this as losing your power but as gaining an ally in whatever you may need in the future. Power is only important if you don't have it. You didn't have it once and gaining it meant the world to you. Now you know what it's like to have it, so assist someone else to feel the same way.

Inverted

Mjölnir inverted is a defense against all things dangerous and deadly. Mjölnir was used to protect Asgard against the giants and at Ragnarök it will be used to kill Jörmungandr, but at a cost of the life of Thor. Sometimes it's necessary to sacrifice yourself for the greater good and at other times it's not. Mjölnir inverted gives you that chance.

In the past Mjölnir inverted left you defenseless. You have been bereft and left for metaphoric dead. It was not the end but it seemed that way at the time. If it had not been for someone else, you would have been lost in the quagmire of despair and depression. Fortunately, you were able to rise above the situation and reach a position where you were able to fend for yourself again and gain a stable position.

This position you bring into the present is tenuous, though, and needs to be strengthened. If you do not understand how you fell into the position and what it took to remedy the situation, you will find yourself in the present reliving that same problem again and again. Learn from your past and keep Mjölnir from afflicting you again.

The present inverted Mjölnir gives you back the defenses you may have lost. You are the embodiment of Thor, fighting evil and keeping the giants from the gates of Asgard. Not only yourself but others will benefit from your strength and wisdom in this situation, and you may rest assured that whatever answer you have to the problem will be the correct one and will be almost unanimously approved and appreciated.

The future inverted Mjölnir, though, is a different story. You have neither the ability nor the desire to be the protector, and you need to be. Forces are building at the walls of your keep, and if you don't do something in the present, the future, well, there might not be a future that you want to be part of.

I know this sounds dire, and to a degree it is, so pay attention *now* to what is going on to preclude disaster in the future. Put up your wards, grip your hammer firmly—even if this is metaphoric—and stride out into the fray ready for battle. You may not want a fight, but you will prevail when the fight comes to you. Do not back down and you will be victorious.

Over

"I'm not worthy." How many times have we heard this in conversation? Either you've said it or someone else you know has said it. Well, guess what? You *are* worthy and so was Thor. Nowhere does it say you have to be worthy to be a god. You have read the stories of these petty, angry, long-lived "gods" and nowhere does anyone say you have to be worthy of anything, which is a good thing because most of them are not. They are the same as humans, or elves, or dwarves, or giants. So why does it stress you so much to think you have to be worthy all the time?

The over piece of Mjölnir is about being worthy. But it's a falseness— something that the movies and comic books have tricked you into believing about Thor's mighty hammer. He has always been worthy of wielding Mjölnir and you are too.

Over past Mjölnir found you arguing about being worthy. Whoever said that you were not did not deserve your loyalty, friendship, and trust. Being worthy is not about what others think. It's about what you think, and you were worthy because, well, because you are. Look back on those moments of self-doubt and cast them away in the present. They are not you and you are better than belittling yourself and your worth.

In the present you are doubting your worthiness. You have come up against something that is greater than you are, and you doubt that you are able to accomplish the mission or project. Because of that, you are in fear that you are not good enough—therefore, not worthy of the trust and responsibility that has been bestowed upon you.

Once again, cast that doubt aside. Worthiness is not something that can be learned or given. You cannot buy being worthy; if you could then all the millionaires and billionaires would be worthy and the rest of us would not. Instead, most of the worthiest people I know have little to no money or other wealth, but they have their soul, their heart, and their intellect. They are worthy and they are the richest people in the nine realms.

In the future you are going to prove that you are not worthy *unless* you do something now to change that. Watch for an impossible request or project that will take everything you have to complete it. When you fail, and you will because even Odin could not accomplish what they are asking of you, you will wonder if you are ever going to be worthy of anything. Put that thought aside. Walk away from those who cast aspersions toward you and know that doing your best, even if you fail, means you have done the most you can. Remember, at Ragnarök the gods will die. They will fight the best they can, but still they will die. Does that mean they are not worthy because they did not succeed? No, it means they did the best they could against overwhelming odds and they lost. There is no loss of worthiness about that. You only lose your worth if you quit.

MUNINN

Odin has two ravens. One is Huginn and he was mentioned earlier in this book. Muninn is the other raven of Odin. His name means *memory* and with Huginn he flies throughout the worlds each day to keep the All Father informed of what is about. Most of what is to be said was already mentioned with Huginn, so suffice it to say that with memory, like thought, one works in conjunction with the other. And Odin relies on both of these daily.

Vert

Vert Muninn is things remembered. Muninn is the raven of memory and his is the best of all the animals. Every day he flies back and tells Odin what he saw from memory. So, too, is the vert piece. It's all about remembering.

When the Muninn piece is in the past vert your memory was good and you remembered things as they were. Unfortunately, you remembered too vividly and that caused you distress and aggravation. Now that those memories are beginning to fade to a dull ache, you can look back on them and analyze them as they should have been analyzed at the time. Take them out and look at them. Dissect them if necessary, but don't put them back in your mind until you have realized that just because you remember them doesn't make them good or bad.

In the present the vert Muninn is a memory of choice. You are dwelling on this memory to the exclusion of all others and it's becoming an obsession. People around you are starting to notice and it's affecting your work, home, and life. Back off of this memory and let it go. Just because you don't think of something all the time does not mean you don't care or don't love. It means you are human, and you are able to compartmentalize your memories where they need to be.

In the future your memories will become more than you want them to be. However, in this case these memories are fond ones, and you are not carrying them around with you to the exclusion of all others. Remember and smile. There is nothing wrong with that. They are your memories. You worked hard for them and you will need them as you go forward, so take them with you and be at peace with them.

Inverted

With everything you remember there is something that you forget. Memories are not always pleasant and even the pleasant ones fade to dark eventually. I have heard it said that the only memories that last are either the very good ones or the very bad ones. In my life I have seen both of these come to pass and agree with whomever told me that years ago. The inverted Muninn is such a situation. Memories come and go, and in this case they go faster than they arrive.

In the past the inverted Muninn saw you make memories faster than you could process them. Most of them were neither stunning nor horrid. They were just day-to-day memories, and try as you might, you just cannot remember them. Don't worry too much about that, though, because the ones that matter, those truly great memories, are still there. You just need to jog them a little to bring them out again. It's like an old sweater you haven't worn in years. When you put it on you remember the last time you wore it and why you never threw it away. Those times are such as this. Now that it's in the past you can enjoy the little things while letting go of the larger ones.

In the present the inverted Muninn is deliberately forgotten memories. There are things that you just don't want to remember. I can think of a few in my past and I'm certain that everyone reading this section can think of a few in their past as well. Let the memories go. You don't need them. They're not doing you any good and for certain they won't help you in your future. For whatever reason you made them in the past, get rid of them now in the present before they become baggage in the future.

You didn't listen to me in the present when I said to get rid of your memories that you didn't need. Now you have memories that are miserable reminders of what you did and try as you might, you cannot get rid of them. Whatever you do, do not use artificial means to eliminate the memories. Drinking, drugs, anything mind-altering is not the answer. Now is the time to confront these memories and quell the demons that they bring back to you. It will take time, believe me, lots of time to do this, but in the end your memories will fade to dark and you will be rid of them once and for all. Trust yourself on this. You can do it.

Over

Muninn wasn't just the raven of memory; he was also a raven that Odin could rely on. Every day the two ravens would fly out over the realms and return each night. That takes commitment and dedication to duty. To think of ravens as just mindless birds is giving them too little credit and giving the two that assist the All Father an insulting amount of distrust.

In the past the over Muninn is the epitome of responsibility. You are like Muninn in that you may be trusted to get the job done no matter what comes before you. Being dependable is the ultimate honor that you have in yourself, and you would die before failing to perform your duty. Most of the time I would caution that, but in this situation that dedication is warranted and necessary for the job at hand. You are the only one who can accomplish this and your passion and zeal for the job and those whom you support show it. Be proud of who you are and what you have done.

The present Muninn over is again the responsible one but for the wrong reasons. You may be responsible and dependable to the wrong people and still do your job. Look at what you are being asked to do and ask yourself if your professionalism and dedication to the operation is being directed in the right place. Just because you swore to do something does not mean that it's right, and just because it seems right does not make it so. Exercise judgement when it comes to your dependability. No one will fault you for saying no if the reasons are not honorable or true. But they will fault you if you don't say no and you do it anyway.

In the future you are going to rely on someone who is not as dependable as you are. You may believe they are, but their words ring hollow and their promises and oaths are easily broken. There is a special place in Helheim for people such as that and they will quickly find themselves there. Don't let them lead you with them. Walk away from those you cannot depend on or trust, and if others ask your thoughts on the matter, be honest and straightforward in your words and actions. Better to tell the truth and hurt those who deserve it than to keep still and abet those who would do you and others harm.

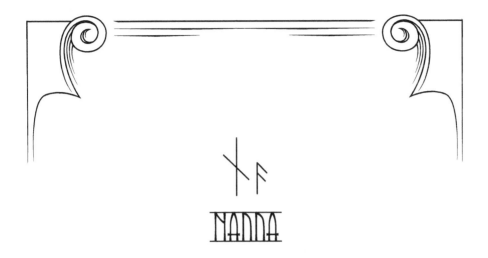

NANNA

Nanna is the wife of Baldr. When Höðr killed his brother, Nanna was so distraught that she died of a broken heart and was placed on his funeral pyre to be with him forever in Helheim. Nanna is the epitome of sacrifice for love. She would not live without her beloved and she basically took her own life in the process; even though she grieved herself to death, she died at her own hand due to her great love of Baldur. For this she is remembered as one of great passion and sacrifice.

Vert

The vert Nanna is love pure and simple. Love means more than anything else and the love of a single person is the greatest joy, and in some cases the greatest pain, there is. Nanna gave everything for her love of Baldr and to that end the vert Nanna piece is such a situation. Whether it is healthy or not to be this much in love is moot. The end result is that's the way you are and you are not going to change.

In the past you have loved deeply, truly, and completely. You have given all you had and have been rewarded with a love in return. It was a glorious love and you remember it fondly. Alas though, it is over, and you long for another such as this. There is a place in your heart that is empty and you wish to fill it. Be of good cheer. Your love will come again, just not the way you expect it.

In the present the vert Nanna finds everyone in love. Well, everyone except you. Your friends, your enemies, the animals around you, and even the plants seem to be in true love, and you are the only one alone. I would like to tell you it will get better, but it might not for a while. Your love is out there but at the moment has no idea you exist. Remain vigilant and resolute that you will find the love you seek and stay positive and forward. Take no insult from those around you who chide you for being alone, nor from those who wish to assist you in finding the love they have. It is all done in good faith and soon it will be your turn to spin the table on them.

It's the future that all is going to come to you. You will know the love you seek when you find it and it will be an all-powerful and consuming love. There will be a mutual love that will fill you both with joy and happiness and you will go into your elder years together.

Inverted

There is a time in everyone's life that we sacrifice for another. It might be our money, our love, our peace, or our life. Nanna inverted is such a time. Sacrifice is all-encompassing for the Norse. One of the greatest gifts someone can give is to give their life for another's. And you will know that when the time arrives. Until then, remain as you are and steadfast in your convictions.

In the past you have taken the high road and stepped aside for another to succeed. The love you should have had went to another and you may not even have known it. Be that as it may, you did the right thing and it was noticed. When score is kept by the gods, you are on the plus side, and when the future comes you will reap the benefits of that score.

The present inverted is the time you have been waiting for. All your sacrifice has come to this. Those whom you assisted in the past have all decided to pay you back at this junction of your life, and that special someone is part of that package. Congratulations. It's been a long time since you have been this happy and it's well justified. And there is *no* other shoe to drop. As you have been reading these chapters you have probably noticed that the gods have a warped sense of humor when it comes to love. They help with one hand and take with the other.

This time, though, there is no one to step in and take it away. Your happiness will remain and even the gods will revel in your pairing. The only one who may destroy all of this is you, so keep a steady hand on the rudder and steer straight and true. Be the love the other needs and you will know bliss.

The future inverted will find you the one being sacrificed for. And it won't be a pleasant experience. Your time is coming, and heartbreak is on the horizon. Where there should be great happiness you will only find bleakness. But then in the middle of your morass someone will step up and sacrifice all for you. You did not ask them to and you did not expect it but there it is, and you must live with it. While you feel that you should have done something differently, remember that it was their fate to do what they did. *And* it was their choice. You were just the recipient of the act and to disrespect it would be a great insult.

Over

Everyone, I believe, has said they would do anything for love. And I believe that you would sacrifice everything you have to experience true love. The Nanna over gives you this chance. You will pay anything for true love and unfortunately that might mean more than you have.

You were lucky in the past. Your loves were inexpensive and easy. You went through your past finding the loves you needed or wanted, and no one was hurt or distressed. You now feel that all the experiences you had in the past were worth it and the price you paid—and some were expensive—was also worth it. You're expecting me to say "no wait, the worst is yet to come," but I'm not going to. There is no downside to your past. It was solid and worthwhile, and you have the memories, and the bills, to show for it. Revel in those memories. Pay the bills and then let them go.

The present is as far away from the past as possible. Nanna over in the present finds you unable to experience love no matter what you do or what you offer. You can't even buy love, and in this day and age that's a hard fact of life. This situation will continue for as long as you believe that money and material wealth are all you need for love.

Love cannot be bought or traded. It's not until you release the belief that money and material wealth are all you need for love that love will find its way to you. Love must be earned and fought for. The term "at any cost" doesn't refer to monetary wealth. It's the heart that pays this debt and it's the heart that must be given. Only then will you find your love, and the cost until then will be expensive.

Finally, in the future love comes for you. You are not looking for it. You've had a rough time with love and if you never find anyone, you say you will be fine with that, but that's a lie, and deep down, you know it. No matter how much you fight the feelings, you are going to experience love, and while it won't cost *you* anything, it will cost the other everything. However, in the end it will be worth the expense and you two will be very happy. All it takes is for you to open your eyes and your heart to what is coming, and when it does, accept it at face value. There is no ulterior motive to this one.

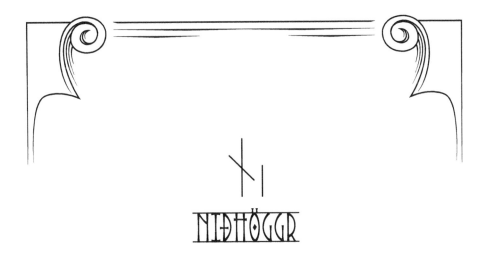

NIÐHÖGGR

Niðhöggr is the serpent that gnaws at the roots of Yggdrasil. He sends insults up the tree to the eagle at the crown by way of Ratatoskr the squirrel. Although Niðhöggr is a destructive entity in the Norse hierarchy, he plays an important role in the rites of the dead. No one knows what he says to Ratatoskr, or if he says anything at all, but when he is not insulting the squirrel or the eagle, he is at the well of Niflheim, where he chews at the roots of the great ash.

He is also responsible for devouring the corpses of the dead at Náströnd. Not only does he do this now, prior to Ragnarök, but he will continue his ritual after the end of the realms and the beginnings of the next.

Vert

Nothing is forever in any world. Stagnation is a misnomer. Everything moves either forward, backward, or to one side or the other. That is the way of Niðhöggr in the vert position. Erosion is constant destruction. It may lead to repair and restoration or it may lead to more erosion, but it is a fact of nature and of life and death. We are born, we erode, and we die. Our bodies and everything around us are in a constant state of change.

It goes without saying, although maybe I should at this point, that no matter what you do, you cannot stop time or death. Your past in vert is just a moving treadmill of hours stretching into days that wore at you until you thought it would go on forever. Well, it won't, but the end is pretty drastic, so let's not look forward to that, okay? In your case, the change is a good thing. You have been growing, not necessarily eroding, although one may look like the other depending on the circumstances and perspective. What you have become is impressive, but not as impressive as what you are going to do in the present and the future. Therefore, take what you are and move forward into your spotlight.

In the present, though, the erosion is wearing on you. Your body hurts and your mind is numb at times. The pressures of the situations around you are overpowering, and you feel that you are being destroyed right down to your soul. In nature when there is massive destruction it is often the case that the area or place changes to meet that destruction, and at times the end result is a new beginning. This is the way it is now.

As you work your way through your present-day scenario you are slowly growing and developing a more powerful landscape, and in that landscape, you are the master of all around you. You will be stronger, wiser, and more adept at what you need and who you want to be. If you are not there yet, you will be. Stay positive and work for that result.

The future is often unknown to us, but the Niðhöggr vert future is well mapped out. Things are in flux and they are in flux for a reason. Your past and present have been experiments and beta tests on you to see what you are made of. The gods are testing you, and you are going to pass with flying colors as soon as you realize that you just need to be you. Stop changing to match the situation. You've done so much for so long in so many guises that no one really knows who you are, even the gods. It's time to work on being one person—the person you are meant to be. Slow down, let the course run, and, yes, there will be some erosion around you, but that doesn't necessarily mean it's for the worse. All will work out if you let it.

Inverted

Heimdallur is not the only entity that works all the time and has eternal duty. Niðhöggr does too. His job, if you call it that, is to consume the bodies of the dead that wash up on his shores. Whether he enjoys the corpses or not is moot. He does what he must for as long as he is destined to. So it is with many humans. We work at something we don't necessarily want until we die, but we do it because it's our job or our passion or even our duty. Inverted Niðhöggr is that duty: eternal, never ending, even after death, and possibly without reward or credit.

You are a credit to yourself and everyone around you. You know what you must do, and you have done it as far back as you can remember. Niðhöggr inverted in the past is a testament to your duty and your patience. Your dedication is resolute and all those around you who know you or of you realize what an example you are to others. Let that adulation wash over you. It does no good to bathe in glory if it's something you had no choice doing. Smile, thank them for their praise, and move on. As the saying goes, "There's nothing to see here."

In the present, Niðhöggr inverted is everyone else doing their duty but you are not doing yours. What's the problem? You know what you have or should do, but you have chosen to ignore that. Pick up the slack and get to work. I know you're tired and bored at what you have to do, but it's your duty to perform these tasks, and if you don't do them then another will have to pick up the slack, and that will add extra work to someone else. Nothing lasts forever and even eternal duty is not really eternal. In this case it just seems that way.

In the future your hard work is over. You have done your duty and performed admirably for so long that you now have the chance to rest and relax. Take that rest and enjoy it. Most of us who are hard drivers never seem to be able to slow down and smell the roses. Granted, when you do smell the roses you sometimes get stuck with the thorns, so maybe you have developed an aversion to that.

If that's the case, then try another tack. Take up a hobby, but don't be obsessive about it. Go back to school for the fun of it. Look up old friends or make new ones. Whatever you do, enjoy it. You have worked long and hard for this and it would be an insult to the gods to waste it.

Over

"You are my anchor and my rock." How many times have you heard that in your lifetime? Well, it's sometimes true, but not always the way you think it is. Niðhöggr anchors the world of the dead by consuming the corpses. It's his duty. Yggdrasil is anchored by its roots and those are in constant danger of destruction by this wily serpent. But in the end the ultimate anchor is you. Remember that when you feel lost or adrift. You are your own captain and your own anchor. When you accept that, all will be better.

In the past you have lost that anchor more than once. You have drifted with the tides and been cast against the rocks on the coast. Without direction you didn't know which way to turn, and it felt as though you would never make landfall. In all that time there was one person who was your rock. That person kept you sane and safe and you lost touch with them as you two aged and drifted apart. It's time to find that person again. Remember, though, that neither of you are who you were. There have been many miles of sea between you, but the time is right to reconnect and rekindle that friendship. If that person is not your anchor, you might very well be theirs.

You have ignored all advice to find solace and tranquility in your past and now you are lost in a mist of the present. There is no magic wand that will clear all the clutter and set you on your way. Your mooring lines are well-worn, and the anchor has not been dropped in many years—and of that you are painfully conscious. It's time to ground and center. Whatever it takes, you must calm yourself *now* and settle all the uncertainty that has plagued you in the past. If you ever needed to find that mystical anchor, this is the time.

You will soon see that it's all worth it. Really. Trust me on this one. In the future, Niðhöggr is going to show you that being dependable and settled is not only the right choice for you but for those around you. In the unsettling times to come, you will be needed more than ever as the clear head and the strong voice of reason. You will need to be more grounded and tied to the docks than ever before. All those around you are in chaos. It's as though Ginnungagap has returned and the over-bubbling chaos of nothingness has taken hold of everyone but you. And it has.

Set yourself right and bring everyone home. You are the lighthouse that will save them, and if you fail, all is lost. But you won't fail, will you? You will take up this challenge and do what you have trained for all your life.

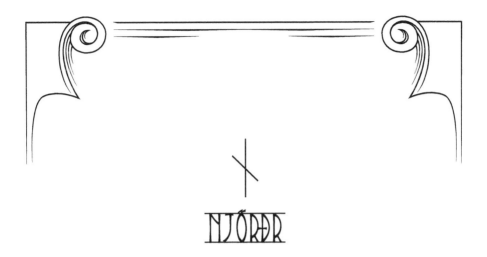

NJÖRÐR

While much of this book has been about the Æsir and the giants, the Vanir also play an important role. During the Æsir-Vanir war, hostages were exchanged. As we spoke about earlier, three of those were the twins Freyja and Freyjr and their father, Njörðr. The mother of the twins could have been Njörðr's sister, Nerthus, but might as easily have been a number of other women of the Vanir or of the giants. Whoever mothered the twins, the three of them moved to Asgard and eventually began being considered gods.

The mother of his children notwithstanding, Njörðr was married, at least for a while. During their travels, Odin, Hoenir, and Loki were responsible for the death of the giant Þjazi, as we talked about in the Iðúnn chapter. After that, his daughter, Skadi, came to Asgard looking for Odin. Skadi was armed in her battle gear and demanded that since the gods killed her father she wanted one of them as a husband. Odin knew that if he refused it would be a dangerous situation, so he acquiesced but put conditions on the husband. The All Father dictated that Skadi could marry any god she chose but she had to choose the god by looking at their feet. In agreement, Skadi added that she must laugh before she left Asgard or there would be war.

As Skadi walked the line of male gods behind a great tapestry with only their feet showing, she found a god with the most beautiful feet she had ever seen. Skadi was convinced that this was the god Baldr because only the most beautiful god could have such alarmingly gorgeous feet. When the curtain was dropped Skadi realized that she had chosen Njörðr. Good to his word and the word of Odin, Njörðr—old, wrinkled, and the god of the sea—agreed to the marriage and Skadi came to Asgard and then eventually to the sea.

The second part of the arrangement with Odin was that Skadi had to laugh. The giantess kept her frown throughout the entire process and into the wedding until Loki took a rope and tied his testicles to a goat. There at the marriage feast, Loki and the goat pulled back and forth, testicles versus goat, until the rope broke and Loki fell into the lap of the new bride. At that point Skadi broke into laughter and the arrangement was completed.

Unfortunately, Njörðr and Skadi could not agree on where to live. Njörðr wanted to live in and by the sea, and Skadi wanted to live in the mountains. Eventually the two separated and now live apart.

Vert

The Njörðr vert piece represents making choices unconventionally. Most of us decide on things using logic and reason. We even draw out decision matrixes: a detailed list of choices and outcomes pertaining to the decision at hand. But at times you end up just making a decision on a whim or on a hunch, or in Skadi's case, on feet.

The vert past piece gives you an idea of what can happen when you choose by hunch or chance. You made a decision that was borne out by neither logic nor reason and you have to live with it. Fortunately, it was not a dire decision and the ramifications won't haunt you for the rest of your life. Learn from this mistake, and next time, look before you decide. And by all means, examine the terms of the agreement. As with Skadi, if she had been more careful in her dealings with the All Father then she might not have been put into the position of marrying Njörðr. Or maybe she would have. It's all the way it is, right?

Njörðr vert in the present highlights your abilities to see things others miss. When you enter into a deliberation, you invariably know who is lying, who is wrong, who is right, what the ramifications are, and how to deal with all of that. Have faith in your gut reaction. Although it's not always correct, it is enough times to be depended on. Your logic is sound and your reasoning secure. You know how to collect data, and when you do make a decision, you are usually correct in your outcome.

The future vert Njörðr cannot make a decision no matter what you do. You are doubting and second-guessing yourself to death. The answer could be staring you in the face and you would doubt it. Let go of your fears and trepidations and trust yourself. There is more to you than you realize, and at this point in your life it's time to count on that.

Even though there is severity in the question at hand, there is also certainty that you will come through with the correct outcome, and even though it may seem unconventional to others, to you it is the most logical and well-thought-out path to the truth. Accept that and go with it.

Inverted

There is a special place in Helheim for oath breakers. It is one of the worst crimes one could commit in the medieval Norse world. The inverted Njörðr takes special consideration for keeping one's oaths or promises. As Njörðr agreed to marry Skadi, so shall all others keep their words, and their deeds will follow. There is nothing more sacred.

Njörðr in the past inverted fails to do just that. Oaths are broken and promises not kept. You are the victim of this, and it has impacted you in ways that you are only now comprehending. Those who broke their oaths should never be trusted again. Even though they were close to you and might have even been family, that is no reason to give them a second chance. Someone who would break an oath once would do it again. Remember that the next time that person comes to you with an idea, offering, or proposition. And never trust them to bear witness.

In the present you need to be careful what you promise because it can and will come back to haunt you. In good faith you offered something without the full knowledge necessary. You were misled, but the deed is close to being done. Stop what you are doing and look around you to ascertain whether or not this is the oath you wish to pledge. It shows no shame to refuse to take an oath, but there is great shame and disgrace once that oath is given and then broken.

In the future oaths are traded like stocks and bonds. People say whatever they need to get the job done and no one keeps their oaths once the deed is done. Do not be one of those people. There are too many already without you adding to the number. Better to keep your mouth shut and your confidence to yourself than to speak and have to break that pledge later. You have been cautioned.

Over

In the over position Njörðr is the piece of jest. Take nothing too seriously. Just as Skadi needed to laugh in order to meet the terms of the agreement, so must you learn humor and mirth to get through the darkness of life.

The past is the past. There is nothing you can do about what you have already done. Worrying about it will help you naught, so laugh about it. Whatever you have done can be lessened by humor. While I don't recommend you tie your genitals to the horns of a goat, you can metaphorically loosen up by seeing the lighter side of the past situation. What's done is done.

Lately you have been locked into a battle between your heart and your head. You know what you needed to do, yet you tarried over it and waited until the situation became so dark and dire that it began affecting you. Look at your feet. What does that mean? Just as Njörðr was chosen as a husband by his feet, you are going to choose with your feet. Go for a walk. On that walk, look to those around you. Smell the air. Pick flowers. Talk to the birds and the animals. Smile at the beauty of nature and the creations of the gods. "There's no time like the present" is something many people say. And do you know what? They are right! Laugh for no reason. Cast all negativity from your mind and start yourself afresh. Let your feet take you places you never thought you could go and revel there.

In the future there will be no mirth. Your world is dark and dangerous. The seas rage and the skies darken. Ragnarök is not yet come but it's the closest you've ever come to it. So, in the present you need to prepare. Take stock of who you have around you that you trust. Weapons are not just of steel and leather. They are of wit and bone. You are the weapon to weather this storm, and with it you will again find your voice and your laugh. It will take a long time and much will pass before you will again be joyous, but that day will come and you will once again revel in the sun.

THE NORNS

The Norns are the three giantess maidens that live at the base of Yggdrasil in Asgard. There they weave the fate of everyone at their birth and hang that tapestry in the great hall.

Whether the Norns are related or not is open to interpretation. In a familial way they would represent grandmother, mother, and grandchild. They may also represent Maiden, Mother, Crone, although that is not mentioned in the literature. What is said, though, is that Urðr, for which the well is named, is the Norn for the past or what has been, Verðandi is the Norn for what is currently or the present, and Skuld is the Norn for what is to come or the future. That would make Urðr the grandmother of the group, or the Crone, using the Pagan connotation. A crone was a woman who had ceased menstruating and became a senior advisor, so to speak.

Verðandi, as the present, is the Mother. She is who gives birth and replenishes life. All need the mother, for without her there is no future, only the past. Finally, Skuld is the youngest since she is yet to be. She is the Maiden who has yet to menstruate and begin her journey into motherhood.

These women water the great tree daily to keep the roots hydrated and spread sand from the edge of the well on the roots to keep the rot from affecting the health of the tree. Even though they do this, the tree suffers from abuse within the branches from the four deer Dáinn, Duneyrr, Duraþrór, and Dvalinn grazing on the leaves and Niðhöggr chewing the roots in Niflheim. The great tree continues to regenerate itself and will flourish until the leaves fall at Ragnarök.

Vert

The past is inescapable. It is gone, never to be returned. Urðr sits on her throne, old and wrinkled, and remembers what it was like back then. Was it better? Was it worse? Do we even know? And does it matter? Well, in that regard, we know the answer. Yes, the past matters greatly. The mistakes you made in the past, unless corrected, will haunt you in the present and doom you in the future.

Vert Urðr is your past, and in that past you are bound by what you did and what was done. There is no going back now. You must live with it and move on as best you can. If it was a pleasant past, then good on ya. If it was not pleasant, then do something about it. Learn from your mistakes and do not make them in the future.

Verðandi is your present vert; it's all about remembering the past. What you did is imperative to who you are and what you are about to be. I cannot stress enough that the past and the present are only separated by a moment. Today is tomorrow's yesterday, so as you move forward you also bring the past with you. Make every moment count since you never get a second chance to change what you have done; you just get to correct it later.

The future vert is Skuld, when you have a chance to fix what you did. You cannot change what you did, but at least you can amend it or not repeat it, depending on whether it was positive or negative. Skuld doesn't care either way. She is too young to understand what you are going through and too inexperienced to know how to help you. It's now up to you.

Inverted

As Verðandi will tell you, there is only one instant of present. To speak of the present as being a great expanse of time and space is to fool oneself. Even the gods may not experience more than a fleeting second of present before it becomes the past. And as they and we age, our past becomes greater than our future. But the present is ever with us. We don't know any other time than now and it's the now that Verðandi looks over.

In the inverted past we thought of ourselves as great and glorious, and Urðr laughed at us for that. We had dreams and ambitions and some of us even accomplished them. But as we aged and grew in our mind and body, we realized that the past is better there. We should not dwell there but know that without the past the present is useless. Therefore, the Urðr position of the Norns is your gateway into the world that was, and you need not do anything other than know it was there and so were you. You cannot go back there. *Remember that!*

Present inverted Verðandi does you neither good nor harm. The present is too short to do much with. And similar to the mother, she is nurturing you through these continual moments so that they become a series of memories. The Verðandi present piece is a place of comfort and peace. It's the better of the times instead of the worst of times, and relish them as you will. Also share them with others that may not be as fortunate as you. If there is a give-and-take in the universe, then for every positive you experience, someone is knowing the negative. Share your positive so that others may know it. And when you do, others will share with you when you need it. Verðandi present is symbiotic.

However, Skuld inverted in the future is anything but peaceful. Here is where you are going to need others. If you have done your part in the universe and given your positive energy to those in need, then you have but to ask and you shall receive. But if you have squandered your positivity, then it will be a long and lonely future.

Over

If you think about it, you never reach your future. No matter how fast you run or high you climb or deep you dive, the future is always one second away from you. It taunts you with its proximity but is never realized. I wonder how many have gone mad knowing they can never hold the future that they so desire.

Urðr in the past over are your regrets. You are rife with them and they do you no good. What you wanted in your future you didn't get. What you did get may or may not have been what you wanted, but it was what you were destined. Accept that, atone for anything you need to, celebrate whatever you wish, and move on.

The present over is an interesting place. Verðandi knows that the present passes so quickly that it's as though it was never there. You are balancing the past and the future on the head of a pin and it's starting to wear on you. Relax. Take a vacation. Read a book. Go out with friends or loved ones. Make memories. These are the times that you will remember when the present has moved far into the future. Now isn't that a thought for the day? Seriously, take the time to enjoy life. You are moving too fast and too frantically and neither is good for you.

The future over is so far away that you should just give up looking for it. Skuld is young, innocent, and too full of herself to be of any use to you. Look closer to home. There is much around you that delights and pleases. Open your eyes to what you see. It won't come this way again.

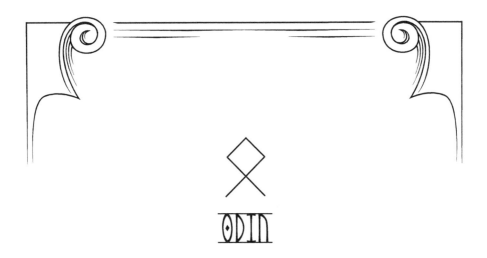

ᚬᛞᛁᚾ

The All Father walks among us. Even though Odin is the ruler of Asgard, he would refuse the title of king; he is often away for long periods of time walking the lands of Midgard and other realms. As the ruler he is the rule maker but often also the rule breaker. He can be petty and jealous as easily as he can be caring and wise.

For a drink of water at Mimisbrunnr he sacrificed an eye. To gain the knowledge of the magical runes he hung on Yggdrasil for nine days and nights. To gain the mead of poetry he tricked his way into a cave.

After the war with the Vanir, the Æsir and the Vanir made a pact to create the wisest human ever. To that end they each and every one spit into a large cauldron and created a human named Kvasir. Kvasir travelled through Midgard and other realms until he came to the home of two dwarves: Fjalar and Galar. The two dwarves killed Kvasir and brewed his blood into mead that had the power of Kvasir and his wisdom. Anyone who drank of the mead gained great skill and fame as a poet and orator.

Once the two dwarves killed Kvasir, they went on a killing spree. First, they killed a giant named Gilling by drowning him in the ocean. After that they killed Gilling's wife by hitting her in the head with a millstone. They would probably have kept on killing if not for Gilling's son, Suttung, capturing them and taking them out to a low set of rocks in the sea to drown at high tide. The dwarves promised anything to be allowed to live and Suttung traded their lives for the mead of poetry. Suttung knew what he had and how powerful it was. He tasked his daughter, Gunnlöð, to protect the jars of mead and shut her up under the mountain Hnitbjorg.

When Odin heard that the mead had been created and then hidden under a mountain, he swore to retrieve it for it was too important to be hidden away from the worlds. He went to visit Suttung's brother, Baugi. When he reached the farm, he told the nine workers in the field that he would sharpen their scythes for them. After he did the servants were able to cut much faster and cleaner and they each wanted the whetstone that Odin had used for themselves since they felt it had magical powers, which it did, but not the way they thought. Odin threw the whetstone into the air and the nine servants killed each other trying to get the stone.

After that, Odin went to Baugi's farmhouse and told the farmer his name was Bölverkr. He told Baugi about the servants killing each other and said that he would perform the work of all nine men for a taste of his brother's mead. Baugi admitted it was not his mead but said if Bölverkr could perform the work of nine men he would do the best he could to help him get a taste of the mead.

At the end of the season the crops were all gathered, and Odin kept his part of the bargain. When Baugi and Odin went to Suttung to ask for the mead, he refused. Being an oath breaker was one of the worst crimes in the nine realms and Baugi knew that. Therefore, Odin and Baugi went to a section of the mountain closest to the cave of the mead so that the promise Baugi made with Bölverkr would be honored. Odin pulled a drill from his cloak and bade the giant to drill a hole through to the cave. It took two attempts, and when the hole was completed Odin turned himself into a snake and crawled into the cave. Once inside he took the appearance of a handsome young man and seduced Gunnlöð. She agreed that if the young suitor would sleep with her for three nights she would grant him three sips of the mead.

After the third night with Gunnlöð, Odin took three sips of the mead. Each "sip" drained the container. He then turned himself into an eagle and flew back to Asgard. Unfortunately, Suttung saw what had happened and turned himself into another eagle and gave chase. Suttung failed to catch the All Father, and Odin spit out the mead from his stomach into the vats in Asgard. While doing that, some was spilled over Midgard and that is why the poets and writers of Midgard are not as good as the ones in Asgard: Midgard only received a little bit of the marvelous mead. It is also interesting that the god of poetry, Odin's son Bragi, was the son of Gunnlöð that Odin slept with under the mountain.

As I said earlier, the All Father travels the nine realms and doesn't always cause chaos or destruction. At times he witnesses it at battles and personal combats. When he travels, he is always with his two ravens Muninn and Huginn. He is also accompanied by his two wolves: Geri and Freki. When in the presence of death by combat, Odin calls upon the Valkyries to take the valorous warriors that died in battle to Asgard to either Valhalla or Folkvang. There the warriors fight and feast, training for Ragnarök.

Vert

Odin is the ruler of all things. He is referred to in a number of ways, and one of those is the All Father, in that he is the father of all things—but is that really true? He did not create the giants. He did not create some of the realms of the universe. However, he did create enough of the worlds to be remembered as the greatest creator of all time, and that's not too bad. Just remember that everything that may be created may also be destroyed.

The vert Odin is a piece of power. Odin is the ruler, as previously stated, and he has the power of life and death in many situations. For this he paid a great price many times, and those who follow him pay a heavy price to do that. But in the end, like the mead of poetry, proximity equates to power.

In the past the vert Odin is that power. You do not have it, but you wanted it so badly that it tainted you to all other paths. And what good did that do you? You lost your friends, your loved ones, and your hope. You are now in the present thinking that it's all over for you, but it's not. There is always hope, and with hope you are never lost. Turn your life around and give up being the one in control. Learn to trust others and they will in turn trust you.

Being the ruler of all things is no longer what it was when Odin started all of this. Even Odin would agree with that.

It's now the present. Odin vert is the power you wanted in the past. You now have it and it's not what you thought it would be. Power over all things is not what it's cracked up to be. There is responsibility, duty, work, and little play. Remember that when you want to be in charge again and think you could be the ruler of all things.

In the future you now know better than to want it all. You have moderation in all things and that extends to your wish for power and control. And that's a good thing since you will be offered more power and charge than you ever imagined. Refuse it. You have enough to keep you busy with your family, your friends, and your work. Even when those close to you that you trust ask you to take on more and even offer you the position of honor, you need to look hard at what they are offering and what it will cost you. Then smile and say no, thank you.

Inverted

Odin did whatever was necessary to gain the wisdom to rule the nine realms. He gave his eye for a drink at Mimisbrunnr and we complain about studying more than ten minutes to learn how to … whatever. We definitely don't have the desire that Odin had, and probably never will. This is what the Odin inverted represents: the insatiable thirst for wisdom.

Your past has been a difficult time for you. Academically you have wanted to go farther than you have, and you have had to work harder than most to accomplish what you have gained. As you sit and look back on that time, you realize that it wasn't the academics that were the problem but your attitude to learning. Learning doesn't come easy to all and few can master something without sweat and toil. It will do you well in your present and future to remember that. You are quite capable of learning and mastering anything you set your mind to, but you must, and I repeat *must*, concentrate on the task at hand in order to gain from it. Odin may have sacrificed his eye for knowledge, but he thought long and hard about it before he plucked out that gift to Mimir, and you should too.

Odin inverted in the present is a great draw for you. There is much wisdom out there in the world and you have all the time now to seek it out and gain it. Slow down and find a steady pace. Nothing is gained by rushing and much is lost. If you want to know or learn something, then patience is the key. Accept that you won't instantly know something and it will come to you faster than if you adopt a know-it-all attitude. Take my word for it; you will get it eventually.

In the future there is much to learn but you have closed your mind to it. In your life you have become jaded to learning since you have not been able to learn and retain at the level you feel you should be at. You have closed your mind to your abilities and that has hampered you in your work and your play. When the time comes—and it will—that you think there is nothing more you can learn and that you are "learned out," take a deep breath and close your eyes. Think of Mimisbrunnr and the cool waters. Then think of Odin's eye at the bottom of the well and be thankful you don't need that much sacrifice to learn what you need. You have what it takes. Use it.

Over

Before Odin sought wisdom above all other things, he was the creator. He and his brothers created seven of the nine realms, the sky, the cosmos, and the races, with the exception of the giants and the Æsir. Without Odin, the universe would be a great chaos of giants and gods. We must remember that when we think of Odin and when we think of him as the creator, we must also think of him as the destroyer, for he destroyed Ymir to create everything else.

In the past over Odin is the great creator and you were too. You had good ideas and they all came to fruition. You should be very proud of yourself for what you have done and what you accomplished. Now, don't sit this one out. Keep at it. After Odin created the other realms, the sun and the moon, night and day, stars, clouds, and people to populate the other realms, did he rest? No, he did not. He created Yggdrasil and then went out to make certain what he made was working properly. So why do you think that you are done being creative? Back to work, but remember to take some downtime too. Burning out is for Ragnarök.

Over present is where you really want to be. You have been successful in your past and your future looks bright and full of possibilities. Take that position and enjoy the moment. People will come to you for advice. Give it to them. Tell them what you really think and not what they want to hear. You have the power to create great things in them if you just trust your instincts and move forward. Even when you think you are wrong, you are not. Unlike most of your friends in this time and space, you have all the answers and everyone wants to be near you because special things are happening around you. Cherish the moment.

In the future the Odin over shows you the flip side of the All Father. You have the ability to both create and destroy. Which will you choose? It's easy to say, "I want to be the creator," but when the time comes you will want to take the easy road and let things fall apart. You might even let them crumble so you can put them back together for more glory. That's ego at a level even the All Father doesn't have. And you shouldn't either.

You will know what is right and what is wrong. You are not a god. You are a human being who cares about their fellow man and you will do the right thing. And if that means letting some things crumble to dust and blow away, then so be it. As I said in the beginning of this chapter, everything that may be created may be destroyed.

RAGNARÖK

Ragnarök will be preceded by three years of winter. The sun will darken and the night will descend upon the lands. Fenrir will shake off his magic ties and roar again, a free wolf. Jörmungandr will shudder until Naglfar loosens its moorings and sails free. Loki shall storm across Bifröst and confront the gods in the final cataclysmic battle. Loki and Heimdallur will fight to the death. Jörmungandr will kill Thor with his venom but will have died first from the mighty Mjölnir. Fenrir will consume the All Father and will die by Vidar, the son of Odin.

Freyjr dies by the flaming sword of Surtr and the fire giant goes on to burn Asgard and Midgard. Baldr and Höðr return from Helheim and become rulers of the new world order after the conflagration. Líf and Lífþrasir will emerge from Hoddmímir's Wood and repopulate the world. Hel will continue to rule over the dead and death will go on as though nothing happened.

Vert

Ragnarök is total and absolute destruction. Entire worlds are destroyed and races all but eliminated. Many often say, "If there is a God, why does this happen?" when we have cataclysmic destruction. Well, in this case there are gods, and this happens because it's supposed to. It's the natural order of the universe to cleanse itself and then start again. This is the cleansing portion of that plan.

Ragnarök in the past vert was your destruction. You have had a tough time and you feel that everything around you is gone. It really wasn't, but there was scant little to find in the aftermath of the terrible situations that overtook you. There is a light at the end of the tunnel, though, but it's just a dim candle. You are still alive. You have that and the will to regain what you lost and prosper when you move into the present. Remember that when you fall silent to dismay late at night after feeling overwhelmed by what has befallen you.

The present vert Ragnarök is little different from the past, except it's not you. Those you love and respect are not doing well, and that is affecting you as though it were you being destroyed piece by piece. Your family is being beset by the forces of Hel and they are buckling under the seemingly insurmountable pressure of the moment. You are at your wits' end to help them and you feel that whatever you do will just drag you into their pit of despair. But if you do nothing then nothing will change. Thor, Odin, Freyjr, and Heimdallur all know they are going to die at Ragnarök. Does that stop them from fighting until the end? No; and it should not stop you. They are your family and friends. They were there when you needed them. They need you now.

The destruction is over by the time you reach the future. Everything that could burn has burned and what could be destroyed has been destroyed. There is nothing left but to pick up the pieces. Do that methodically and with intent. Any haphazard plan will fail and you will be back where you started from. I'd like to say that you are ready to begin again but that would be presumptuous. You still have things to clean up before you can regroup, so take your time and get it right. It matters in the end.

Inverted

With everything that ends, there is a new beginning. The inverted Ragnarök is that new beginning. The worlds have been decimated, burned to a crisp by Surtr, and what is left is death and destruction. But at that point new life begins with Líf and Lífþrasir in new Midgard, the sons of Thor, Baldr, and Höðr in new Asgard, and Njörðr back in Vanaheim. These will bring life back to the realms, and with that new life will be new deaths and Hel will be there to usher in the ever-present dead, feeding the more heinous to Niðhöggr.

The past inverted is where it all ended and began again. Your world crashed down but you were able to pick up the mantle and carry on. Yay, you! It takes a lot to look Fenrir square in the snout and laugh. You did it and you should be proud of that. Well, don't get too proud; there's always tomorrow.

In the present the newness has worn off. You are feeling as though it wasn't enough, and that can be debilitating if you are trying to get yourself and others back on track. Stop and take stock of your inventory, not just your physical things but your mental abilities as well. You are not the person you were when you lost it all. You are now stronger, smarter, and with a different sense of purpose. That counts for quite a bit in this world, and what you do with all these new talents will set you up for future successes.

In the future the inverted Ragnarök is going to be the same as what you just survived unless you do something *now*. Just because you started over doesn't mean you started better. You must learn from the mistakes of the last destruction and apply them to the future you want. If you don't, and you let the same occurrences repeat themselves, then you will be looking for another restart later. And possibly another one after that until you learn from your errors. There are too many ways to fail in this world. You don't have to try every one before you succeed.

Over

One of the fun parts of divination is that you are looking for what is to come. You don't know your future and you are relying on the cards, stones, pieces, tea leaves, whatever, to get you there. With Ragnarök, everything is already laid out for you. There is no mystery of the future or what is to come. When you begin to explore the end-times then you realize that whatever you do has already been forecasted; however, you don't know what affects you, and that's an important difference.

The Norns have laid out your future and how it will play out. Ragnarök has been foretold for a thousand plus years, but you, my friend, are still new to this. You have no idea what is going to happen in your life and that's the joy—and at times the misery—of the world. Accept the newness of the situation and revel in it. Know that whatever is to come will come, but if you do nothing then nothing may be your outcome. You have the chance to create your world, even though it may already have been written. However, you are not a god and you cannot see the great tapestries. Therefore, you have no idea what your fate is so you may do as you wish, and if the Norns so desire, they may reweave your future as a reward for a life lived well. As they say, "If you concentrate on the destination, you miss the journey."

In the past you knew it all. You were young and at times foolish, but you were young and that's the point of all of this. The young know everything. Well, they really don't but they think they do and that's good enough for them. It isn't until it's too late sometimes that we realize that not only do we not know everything, but we actually know darn little of anything. We have all gone through this, though, so don't dwell on it. You were foolish and you got over it. You did get over it, didn't you? If not, then there is no hope. You'll just have to keep going through all of this until you figure it out since the rest of us really do know everything.

In the present you now know what you don't know, and that's pretty much still everything. The difference between the present and the past is that you are older and wiser. You still don't know what you need to, but you know enough to start learning what is out there since it's all there if you know or discover where to look. Be an explorer. Eventually become one of the few who really do know everything, or at least enough to make others think you know it all.

The future has already been written; you just don't know what it is. You are a pawn in a game and the game is rigged against you. The best you can do is ride the waves and try to figure out the rules before the next move. Death is your opponent and death really does know everything. And if you lose, then you lose life and that means … you get the idea, right?

So, in the future you are going to study everything you can. Play the game of life as though it was your last game ever, which it is, and eventually work out that even though some know everything, the best you can do is to know enough about enough to know you don't know everything about everything.

RATATOSKR

Ratatoskr is the squirrel who runs up and down the trunk of Yggdrasil carrying insults and taunts between the unnamed eagle at the crown and Niðhöggr at the roots. He is basically a messenger for the dwellers in the tree but is reported to also cause chaos within the branches.

Vert

Ratatoskr is a messenger, but not of the gods. He is a singular entity and in that respect acts independently of anyone or anything else in the cosmos. What he says to the great eagle and Niðhöggr, no one knows. Suffice it to say, it is enough to cause dissention in the tree and pleasure to the squirrel.

In the past you have received news that has been less than pleasant. It caught you off guard and you had no comeback for it. The individual who delivered the news was not your friend and you always suspected that he was not completely trustworthy nor the information accurate. You were right on each of those counts.

Those who believe what others say without a second opinion or collaboration take the risk of being offended, insulted, or hurt by things that are not always what they appear to be. That was the result that time. It's now time to let that go and move on. Whether you researched the truth or not was up to you, but whatever you did, walk away from the situation now.

In the present Ratatoskr vert has you in the messenger position. You have information that you need someone else to know. The only problem is that the person who needs to know it is neither your friend nor someone you want to associate with. You must find a third party to act as a go-between. Like Ratatoskr running back and forth up and down Yggdrasil, you must now find your own squirrel, vet that person to be certain they can be trusted, and then let them loose to deliver the message. It is a dangerous game you will undertake, and it can go wrong on many levels, so be careful and trust only those you must.

In the future vert the squirrel is quiet. There is no news that you are waiting for and you are concerned by that. You have waited enough time, you think, and now you wish to act. Do not! Trust the squirrel to bring the information you are waiting for since nature, and messengers, often move at their own speed. To force the issue would cause more damage than even you can anticipate. Patience is the key to this piece.

Inverted

Ratatoskr is not just a messenger; he is an instigator. He uses his role as messenger to cause dissention up and down Yggdrasil. And as he does, he keeps trouble stirring much as Loki does to the gods in Asgard. A parallel could be drawn between Ratatoskr, the eagle, and Niðhöggr and Thor, Loki, and the giants. Both are diverse groups with a rampant instigator in the middle.

Past inverted Ratatoskr really is all about you. You were the disobedient child, even though most people thought you were the best of the group. You manipulated everyone else to get them in trouble and then you sat back and watched the ensuing chaos. I hate to tell you that it's about to come to a head. Those who were the brunt of your chides and jabs are now older, stronger, and wiser, and you are still trying to manipulate them as you did when you were younger.

It's time to grow up and become an adult, no matter what age you are. Even Loki learned that being the instigator in the middle of the fight has its downside. In fact, he relearns it every time the bowl fills and Sigyn must pour out the venom. That venom is building above you and you need to remember that.

Congratulations. Whether you listened to me about your past or not is irrelevant. The fact that you have cleaned up your act and you no longer instigate others in the present just to please you is a positive sign. It shows that you can learn and apply lessons to yourself as well as others. It's now time to repair the bridges that you burned while you were being, well, not being nice. (You expected me to say something else, didn't you?) Pay back those you hurt with interest. They are soon to become people you will rely upon as you go into your future, and if you continue as you have you won't have anyone to watch your back.

Warning for the future! There are those out there who have not learned the lessons you have. They are still causing chaos at others' expense and you are in their crosshairs. A second warning is in store. Those who you are certain will be the ones to cause you harm are the least of your problems. There is an old saying: "Keep your friends close and your enemies closer." In this case, it's your friends that you need to worry about. They are the ones who will start your problems and they will be the ones who will benefit from them if you don't guard yourself early and well. The future really is all about preparedness.

Over

Ratatoskr is not just about being a messenger or an instigator. It's about the chaos that ensues when he gets his tail up and starts chatting up animals that neither like nor want to get along with each other. I believe that if they could, both the eagle and the serpent would rend the squirrel apart, but he is faster than them and keeps moving. The chaos he creates, though, stays long after he leaves the area.

In the past over the squirrel leaves a mess wherever he lands. He is the epitome of chaos and you are often the recipient of that mess. The problem is, you are too accepting of his behavior and you think you can change him. You know who I'm talking about, so don't deny you've enabled your squirrel too long. Put your foot down and deal with the problem causer. If you don't, then he will keep at it until he has destroyed you and moved on to someone else.

Your present is a better situation. You have learned to deal with your chaos and there seems to be a calm about you. That calm will be shattered if you are not careful. Watch out for others who have not yet rid themselves of Ratatoskr and still think he is a cute little squirrel. Just because people allow chaos into their life doesn't mean they enjoy it. Sometimes, though, they don't know anything else and having the chaos is better than being without it. You, fortunately, are not one of those people. Chaos is for others. You can and will rise above it.

The future over will be chaos free. You have finally rid yourself of everyone and everything around you that has caused, or will cause, you trouble. You have weeded the gardens of everything toxic and your fences are strong and tall to keep out any animal, even that pesky squirrel, who might try to enter your keep. Enjoy your time. You worked hard and long for it and deserve it.

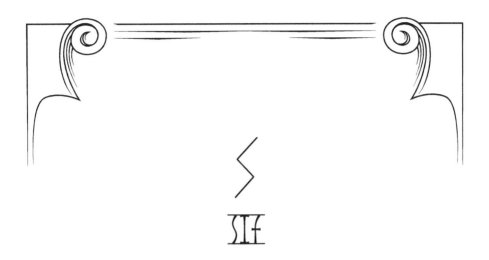

Sif

Sif is the queen of the fields and golden-haired goddess married to Thor. She is the mother of Þrúðr with Thor and of Ullr with an unknown god. She is written about because of her long blond hair that is her prize possession.

In the sagas Loki, in a fit of mood, cut off all of Sif's hair as she lay sleeping. When Sif awoke she was so embarrassed that she refused to leave her chambers. Thor hunted down Loki and threatened to kill him if he did not remedy the situation that he caused. Loki went to the dwarves in Svartalfheim and convinced the dwarves there to spin a new head of hair from the finest of gold. Loki saved his life and Sif her pride with this feat, and the gods continued in their pursuits.

Sif is thought to be one of the goddesses of the fields due to her blond hair, and the story of the cutting of her locks is thought by some to be a metaphor for the harvesting of the grains. Be that as it may, Sif is honored by the farmers as one of their patron goddesses of the harvest.[41]

---

41. H. R. Ellis Davidson, *Gods and Myths of the Viking Age* (London: Penguin Press, 1965), 84.

Vert

The golden harvest in the fall ensures a plentiful larder during the winter. Without the harvest the animals die, the people die, and the nation dies. These are the things that Sif offers in the vert position. She is the bountiful queen of the fields and she is the metaphor for the reaping of the grain. Without her there is nothing and no one thrives.

In the past you were bountiful and full. You had it all and everything you touched turned to gold. Relax, it's not going away. You are still in control of everything you worked for, and you are bringing it with you into the present where it will multiply and replenish greatly. You worked hard for what you have, and you have a right to keep it.

When Sif is in vert in your present you have a difficult decision to make. You have had little in the past and now you have the opportunity to greatly increase your holdings. You know how to do it and you have the resources to accomplish it. The only problem is that to succeed, someone else must fail. Do you have what it takes to cause harm to someone else in order for you to progress? I'm not here to make that decision for you. It's something you will have to wrestle with and whatever decision you make will be with you for the rest of your life.

The future vert Sif looks rosy and bright. It looks like you will get everything you desire and your farm and fields will be overflowing. It looks that way even though it is not. There are stones in your fields. Mice run rampant in your bins and your grain suffers. Your cattle and sheep are ridden with worms and the milk is soured. But it looks like everything is rosy and bright.

That's the problem with how things look and how things actually are. It's going to be up to you to see through the allure of the golden harvest to the ragged and dire truth of the situation. It could be as bad as you think it is. It could be far worse. Or, to fix the problem you might just need a little medicine, a few cats, maybe a short talk with Freyja, and time. Whatever it is, it's now up to you.

Inverted

We all must be prepared. And to be prepared takes work, lots of hard work. It's not enough to say, "I am ready for whatever" and have that proven out. You must actually *be* ready and that takes preparation. Sif in the inverted is that preparation. It's the work and the toil of preparing the fields, soaking the seeds, keeping the rows clean of weeds and moist enough to grow. It's the preparation of honing your scythe sharper than anything Odin could and still being strong enough to swing it hour after hour. And in the end, you will prosper for that.

In the past you have always been prepared. Almost like the over-ambitious Boy Scout, you have kept everything ready for any occasion. And when you needed it, you had it. Be of good cheer that you did that because it will take you into the present with enough to get you through.

The present Sif inverted is, again, the well-prepared farm and house. You are knowledgeable in your craft and those around you are envious of what you know but appreciative of what you share with everyone. No one faults you for your successes and everyone celebrates with you. Even when you fail, and everyone does from time to time, your failures seem to be fewer than most. That's because, of all those around you, the one thing you have always been is prepared.

Future Sif continues the trend of being prepared. While others are wandering around aimlessly looking for a direction, yours is set and true. Even in a cloudy sky, your ship sails forward safely and swiftly. Keep the momentum and you will know success far into the future, where everyone will know your name and your fame.

Over

As we have seen throughout this book, if there is one side there is another. With Sif, she is bountiful harvest, but she is also bareness and depletion. You cannot expect one without the other.

In the over past you have been without and you know what that feels like. It's not something you ever want to experience again, and you have taken every precaution to eliminate the possibility. You have been successful. The emptiness that you have suffered has been abated and you are now feeling the joy of rebirth and fullness. Enjoy that for as long as it lasts. You might expect me to say that it will end soon, but that's up to you. If you keep your wits about you and your eyes firmly on the future, you can ride what you had in the past well into your golden years.

The present is also a possibility for ending your drought. Rains come and rains go, but droughts are unforgiving and may go on for years. Look at the great drought of the thirties that turned the Great Plains into a dust bowl. No one could have foreseen this, and no one was prepared for it. Sometimes disasters happen without any warning and you just have to plan for them. Think of Sif inverted and be prepared. It may or may not alleviate any situations that arise, but at least you will be better off than if you did nothing.

The future is no place to be. Live in the present for as long as you can. Sif over in the future is one of emptiness. Therefore, remain in the present and live every day for that day. We have talked about the future never coming since every day is the present. Be that situation. Let others live in the future. You need to live in the now, where it's warm and sunny. Let the future be dark and gloomy without you.

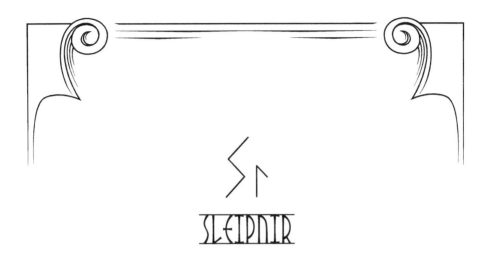

SLEIPNIR

Sleipnir is one of the most unusual animals of the Norse arena. And considering it also contains a giant wolf and a serpent large enough to bite its own tail while encircling Midgard, that's a pretty powerful boast. And it's not just his physical description that makes him so unique but also his pedigree.

Sleipnir is a product of Loki in the form of a mare and Svaðilfari, the steed of the anonymous stonemason who offered to build a wall around Asgard in one season in exchange for the hand of Freyja in marriage and the sun and the moon. Since Loki drew Svaðilfari away from the work site, the unknown mason was unable to complete the task and was killed.[42] In the end Loki bore a foal with eight legs named Sleipnir and he was gifted to Odin as his battle stallion.

Sleipnir is borrowed by Hermoðr after the death of Baldr. Hermoðr rides for nine nights and more to confront Hel in Helheim to ask for the release of Baldr from the dead. Finally, Odin rides Sleipnir into the land of Jotunheim,

---

42. Seigfried, ed., *The Illustrated Völuspá*, 48–51.

where he meets Hrungnir. At the house of the giant, Odin says his horse is faster and finer than any other horse in the nine realms. When Hrungnir challenges Odin to a race, he mounts his steed Gullfaxi. Odin leads Hrungnir all the way from Jotunheim to the gates of Asgard, where he loses the wager.

Vert

Horses are all about riding and work. One is for pleasure and one isn't. (I have always wondered if either was pleasurable for the horse.) Sleipnir in vert is one of travel. There is no physical labor that does not involve the horse. Whether you are journeying for pleasure or work is up to you. The horse will do the same work either way. Remember that when you plan your next ride.

In the past you wanted to travel but never did. You looked at all the travel brochures, talked to travel agents, looked online for specials, and every time you were ready to pull the lever and go you changed your mind. It's time to ask yourself, "Do I really want to travel?" If the answer is yes, then get on with it now. There is no time like the present.

In the present the vert Sleipnir has you actually travelling. Congratulations, you finally listened to me for a change. I was beginning to feel as though I was just writing to see myself in print. How did it feel? Did you have a good time? That bad experience you had, did it put you off future travel or did you see it as a learning experience?

In the future is when you will come into your own as a traveler. Look forward to this. You have worked long and hard to be able to travel and see things that are new and strange to you. And remember that if you miss something on the first trip you can always schedule another one.

Inverted

Every journey has two parts: the first half is the outbound, the second and equally important is the return. You cannot go anywhere and not return, even if you return to a different place than where you started. Even life is a journey of two parts: you are born, part one, and you die, part two. What happens in the middle is secondary.

Your past has had a number of missteps when you were trying to return from your journeys. Just because everything worked well getting you out the door, you seem to have bad luck getting back home. It's not a curse or karma.

It's just the way things worked out. Go with it and don't take it personally. Sleipnir inverted in the past was a less-than-pleasant time. You really should have planned better when you travelled but at least you got back in one piece, which is more than you can say for some who went with you. However, that is history and a memory, at least to you. To those others that trip is still etched in their minds, and remember that when you try to get them to go again. This time around, you will have to be more convincing that there won't be storms, plagues, and disasters too many to mention.

Sleipnir inverted in the present has you returning to accolades and cheering crowds. You have been away a long time, and everyone missed you. You even missed you. Things have changed and so have you, but none of that matters at the moment. You are home and everything is right with the world. Or so it seems.

The future gives you the chance to plan everything perfectly. Not only will your start be smooth, but your course will be right and your return will be perfect. These are good times to be on the road, the sea, or in the air. Nothing will go wrong as long as you are cautious, but that goes without saying most times. And wherever you go there will be people there glad to see you and welcome you into their homes and their lives. Live the life you have dreamed of and enjoy the ride.

Over

When Odin rides into battle, it's on Sleipnir. The eight hooves flash across the sky and no horse ever born can match the steed of Odin. I won't say that Odin is invincible atop Sleipnir, but he certainly spends a lot of time on him and an equal amount of times winning battles, changing destinies, and sending his Valkyries amongst the dead.

In the past over Sleipnir has been there for you. You have had great success in battles, actual and metaphoric. There was little that you wanted for, and thanks to Odin's great warhorse you were able to accomplish everything you set out to do. At each success I hope you thanked Odin for the use of his steed and the steed himself. If not then, now is the time to do it.

Set out an altar for Odin and Sleipnir. Include mead, oats, water, and bird food for the ravens that always accompany the All Father. Burn a red candle for continued successes in battle, and even if you have not pledged yourself to the All Father, at least offer your thanks to him for what he has allowed you to do with his horse.

The present continues your success in all things. Sleipnir is almighty when it comes to battles, and with him as your war mount you are also. Take care, though, to not overextend yourself, but if you are cautious and watch your supply lines and flanks you will continue to dominate the world in whatever you attempt. Press on, noble warrior. You are doing what you have always thought you could.

Watch out for the future over Sleipnir. You are still going to flourish in whatever you endeavor, but the fight will be a little bloodier and a little more prolonged. Gone is the instant success. Now it's time to plan a campaign instead of just a simple quick battle. Watch your flanks and make certain your shield wall is solid and your companions do their part to cover your head and back. With the support of those around you, you will continue to rise above all the others and push forward to greater things. Well done.

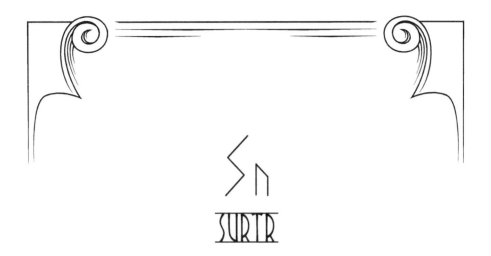

SURTR

Surtr was there at the beginning and he will be there at the end. It was his realm, Muspelheim, that clashed with Niflheim at the beginning of the chaos in Ginnungagap. He is the leader of the Eldjotnar, the fire giants that will destroy everything at Ragnarök. And Surtr will burn Midgard and Asgard to the ground after killing Freyjr. Surtr is possibly married to Sinmara but there is little evidence of this other than obscure references in the *Fjölsvinnsmál*, so the marriage is given little credence.[43]

Vert

Surtr is the creator. Although Odin created more than anyone else in the cosmos, Surtr was there when Buri was created and the Æsir came to be. Therefore, he gets the credit for being the first creator. And in that role, he is primary. He was there when it all began.

---

43. Andy Orchard, *Dictionary of Norse Myth and Legend* (London: Cassell, 1997), 44.

Vert in the past is the memory of the beginning. Surtr was there and so were you. You remember so much of your past that it haunts you at night. You wish you could put it all behind you, but you cannot and that's a good thing. You were created to do great and glorious things and it's in your past that you learned the necessary lessons.

Never forget what you learned and how you became who you are. Your family and friends shaped you into who you are, and you in return are shaping your world around you. Cut through the frost of the chaos and emerge to be everything you were meant to be.

The present finds you as the artist. Creativity and creation are your friends and you are adept at both. You write, sculpt, sing, and dance. There is nothing you cannot do if you put your mind to it. Just as Surtr was there in the beginning to oversee the chaos, you are taking that chaos and molding it into things that are grand and beautiful. Take pride (but not too much) in what you do and offer it to others. Their pleasure will be yours.

The future Surtr finds you in the enviable position of being the grand master of those around you. You are venerated. You are worshipped. And you are humbled by the number of things that you still do not know or cannot do. Never stop learning, creating, or doing. Leave a legacy. It's the greatest gift anyone can give.

Inverted

In my book *Fangs and Claws* I write that there is a saying: "To know everything you must live forever, and no one lives forever."[44] Surtr may be the exception to this saying. He was there at the beginning and he will be there at the end. He has seen everything that has happened between those times. Can you imagine what it must be like to know and to have seen so much?

Well, you've tried, haven't you? You have spent every waking moment trying to experience everything you can. You read, learn, study, and practice. But what has it gotten you? Accolades? You don't care. Degrees? You have enough, really. Knowledge? How much can you take in? It's now time to put everything you've learned into practice. Let the past be the past.

---

44. Gypsey Teague, *Fangs and Claws* (Scott's Valley, CA: CreateSpace, 2012), 176.

And the present is the perfect place to put all that knowledge and experience to work. Surtr in the present gives you the opportunity to be the know-it-all for a good cause. You have worked so hard for so long for this moment. Now is your chance to shine. You are needed. Go out and teach others. Be an example of what a teacher can and should be. And even if you don't think you can teach—teach anyway. Everyone has a different style. Some lecture. Some rant. When I taught high school I tried to make every day relevant to the students. Did it work? I'd like to think it did, but if I even reached one student a day then I felt as though I had accomplished something. Go out and look for that one student. That's all it takes.

The future is going to see you resting, with those you taught doing all the heavy lifting. You can only learn so much or teach for so long before you have to let the next generation carry on. Now is your time to oversee the next crop of teachers, scholars, and philosophers. Be proud of what you did and trust that you performed your tasks flawlessly.

Not only is Surtr the creator but he is the destroyer. At Ragnarök he will take his flaming sword and burn Asgard and Midgard to the ground, destroying all before him. It is his fate to do that and he will with abandon. All will fall before him.

Right or wrong, during the Civil War the Northern General William Tecumseh Sherman burned his way through Georgia. In your youth, you tried to emulate him with your actions and words. Your past is littered with the bodies of those whom you have burned and destroyed. And what has it gotten you? Destruction is part of nature, but wanton destruction for the sake of destruction is just barbarism. It's time to atone for what you have done and heal those wounds that you have created. Just as Ragnarok has a new beginning, it's now time for you to find yours.

In the present Surtr is telling you to begin ridding yourself of baggage. Destruction is an odd creature. It can be all-consuming or it can be isolated and targeted. In your present it's time to be targeted and eliminate everything that is holding you back. You are more powerful than you can imagine. The only thing keeping you from realizing that is you—oh, and your baggage. Follow the example of Surtr and with your flaming sword burn all that is no longer needed in your life. The new vistas at the end of this conflagration will be earth-shattering and you will emerge a new and more powerful person for the experience.

The future will give you the chance to push through the destruction to the new Asgard. You have been cleaning house for so long that you doubt there is much left, and you would be correct. Now is the time to enjoy that cleanliness. The new you awaits, and that you is amazing and without equal. Look back at what you have cast aside and celebrate what you have before you. The time is now.

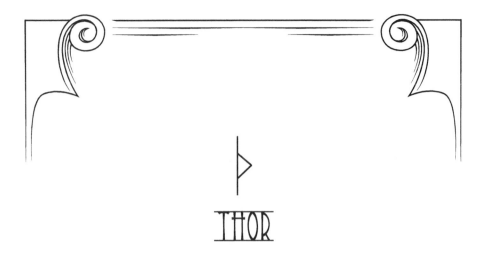

ÞOR

There is only one god of thunder and that god is Thor. Born of a giant mother and the All Father, Thor is the defender of Asgard and the hammer of the gods, figuratively as well as literally. Thor is described by all as tall, muscular, with long hair of a reddish-blond hue, beard, and mustache. While he is wise in some areas, he is not overly intelligent at times and is easily led astray by Loki.

Thor is married to Sif and they have one child, a girl named Þrúðr. He also has two sons, Magni and Móði, by the giantess Járnsaxa. It will be these two sons who will carry Mjölnir after Ragnarök.

Thor is worshipped by many as the patron god of war in the Northern traditions. Those who pray to him or pay tribute to him for fortune wear a small amulet shaped like his hammer, often referred to as a "Thor's hammer." At the National Museum of Iceland in Reykjavik, there is a small bronze statue of a cone-hatted figure holding what looks like a hammer. This statue was found in the northern region of Iceland at the Eyrarland farm near Akureyri. It dates to the eleventh century and is the only bronze statue of its kind ever found in Iceland. I will probably go to a special place in Helheim for this, but I can't help but call this statue The Little Guy. When I first saw it in 2014 at the National Museum of Iceland, it was so small and perfect.

So far in this book we have recounted many tales of the thunder god but there are still a couple left to tell. One such tale involves Mjölnir and how he lost it. Once, Thor found that his hammer had been stolen. Loki offered to help find the hammer and borrowed Freyja's cloak of falcon feathers to fly high in the sky to look for it. Figuring the giants must have stolen it—always blame the giants—Loki flew to Jotunheim to the castle of Thrym, one of the chieftains of the giants.

Thrym freely admitted he did have the hammer safely hidden where no one but he could get to it. He told Loki that he would give it back to Thor in exchange for the hand of Freyja in marriage. When Loki returned to Asgard and informed Thor of the situation, they sought out the council of Heimdallur. Heimdallur suggested that Thor dress as Freyja and Loki as a bridesmaid.

Once at the giant's castle, Thor and Loki were hosted to a feast. Thor, in typical Thor fashion, ate a full ox, eight salmons, and all the food that was offered the other women in the giants' bridal party. When Thrym commented on this feat, Loki explained that "Freyja" was so nervous with anticipation at marrying the giant that she had not eaten in five days. This was her way of releasing that anticipation.

Thrym then tried to kiss the bride, but when he lifted the veil covering Thor's face, the giant saw the red hatred in Thor's eyes. Taken aback, Thrym said never had he seen such piercing eyes. Loki quickly said that "Freyja" had also not been able to sleep and her eyes were red with love for the giant. Thrym was satisfied that he was about to marry the beautiful Freyja and called for Mjölnir to be brought to the bride in preparation for the wedding.

Once Thor had his hammer in his hands, he killed Thrym first then all the other giants at the hall. After that, he and Loki went back to Asgard, where he warned anyone against telling the story of Thor the bride ever again.

Earlier I said that Thor had already encountered Jörmungandr prior to Ragnarök. Thor was a guest of Hymir one day and travelled a long distance to get to the feast. When he arrived, he was so hungry he killed and ate two of Hymir's three oxen that were to be used the next day for the feast. Thor felt badly about that, and the next day he and Hymir went fishing using the head of the third oxen as bait. When Thor hooked a big fish, he began to pull it in. When the head of Jörmungandr surfaced, Thor knew he had what he had come for. As he fought the Midgard Serpent, Thor's feet broke through the bottom of the boat and the boat began to sink. Hymir was afraid of drowning and cut the line, releasing the serpent. Thor was so angry that he threw Hymir into the ocean, swam back to shore, and went home to Asgard.

Another tale of Thor we started earlier. When Odin raced Sleipnir against Hrungnir's steed to Asgard, Odin won and Hrungnir entered Asgard right behind the All Father. He and Odin began drinking and as Hrungnir grew more and more drunk he became more and more obnoxious. First, he said he would take both Freyja and Sif back to Jotunheim with him. Next, he said he would drink all the wine in Asgard. The more he boasted, the more tired Odin grew of this drunk.

When Thor returned to Asgard, he took in the situation and prepared to kill the giant with his hammer. Hrungnir accused the thunder god of cowardice because the giant was unarmed. The challenge was accepted and the two met in a field between Asgard and Jotunheim. Thor had his hammer and Hrungnir carried a stone shield and a giant whetstone as a club. Thor threw his hammer and Hrungnir threw the giant whetstone. The stone struck Thor's head and a piece stuck in his forehead. Mjölnir struck the giant's head and his head was crushed, ending the fight.

With a piece of the whetstone still in his head, Thor went to see Groa, a magic worker who was said to be able to remove the stone. As the stone was being removed, Thor told Groa that her husband would soon be returning, having been with Thor recently. Groa was so excited that she forgot all about the stone in the god's head and rushed out to prepare for her husband's return. That is how Thor still has a piece of the whetstone in his head and will have it until Ragnarök.

Even though Thor is a god, he at times needs some assistance in wielding Mjölnir. To assist Thor in using Mjölnir, he has his belt of power: Megingjörd. This belt doubles the god's strength when worn. He also has a pair of iron gloves called Járngreipr. While not essential to handling Mjölnir, the gloves assist the god in the grip of the shortened handle due to the interference of Loki as the hammer was being created by the dwarves.

Vert

Thor is the protector of Asgard. He is the power behind the throne, so to speak. He uses his hammer as well as his great strength for the good of the gods and will die defending them at Ragnarök.

In the past you have tried to be like Thor. You have fought for the "little guy." Where there was a problem, you were there to intercede as best you could. Even though you were unsuccessful at times, you still did your best to assist those in need and you should be very proud of that. Many that you've never met know you because of the great things you have done.

The present Thor vert exemplifies the attitude that whatever it takes to resolve the situation in the best possible way must be attempted. You are a living god at this point, helping out where you can and doing what you might for those who cannot fight back. Giants come in many sizes and shapes, and in this day and age there are plenty of giants to go around. You are doing your best to take out every one you feel is unworthy, whether they are corrupt bankers, politicians, scam artists, or thieves. You are the wielder of the hammer. However, be careful. Even Thor dies. Choose your battles carefully, and when your feet go through the bottom of your boat it's time to swim to shore and rest. You'll understand this when it happens.

The future holds no rest for you. You have now been tilting at windmills for so long that you don't know any other way. I would recommend that you rest and let others take up the steel gauntlets and magic belt, but you would not hear of it. You will fight the good fight until your last breath and that will make you happy, so who are we to dissuade you?

Inverted

One thing you can say about Thor is that he is quick. He is quick to anger, quick to react, and quick to fight. Usually he is angry at the giants, reacting quickly to something the giants do to anger him, and quick to fight the giants—trying to kill as many as he can, even though his mother is a giant, his father is half giant, and his grandfather is half giant. As I said, Thor isn't always that bright.

Inverted in the past, you were quick as Thor in all of these areas. And it got you nowhere positive. It's good that you changed your ways before you wore yourself out fighting giants that you could never defeat. Look back on those days and see the folly of being so quick to judge and to argue. Learn to take your time in decisions. The wise man chooses both his words and his actions carefully. The foolish man chooses both poorly and suffers.

The present Thor has shown you that being quick or first is not always right, but at times you can be both. You have no giants to slay today. Tomorrow looks good too. Maybe in the future there will be giants but not today or tomorrow. Therefore, take a break, ease into the day, and try not to dwell on what could be. Yes, there might be giants soon, but at the moment there are none and that's a good thing for you. You need the rest.

I was right about the future. There are giants. Giant problems, giant projects, giant challenges, and just you to slay all of these. Would Thor back down and go home? *No!* And neither will you. Your future is bright even though there is much to do and there are many giants to dispatch. Stay your hand and pace yourself. There will always be something to do or a giant to slay, and if you overextend yourself quickly there will be little left of you when you are needed.

Over

If there was one thing in the nine realms that Thor hated more than giants, it was Jörmungandr. He sought out the serpent when he could and tried to kill it but was thwarted. And at Ragnarök he went straight to Jörmungandr and died for it. That is the epitome of obsession.

You've known that obsession in the past. It has done you no good and cost you greatly. Even now, in the present, you are paying a heavy price for the things you should have walked away from but didn't. Don't be like Thor. Learn from your mistakes and leave obsessions to the obsessed. You have neither the time nor the energy for such activities anymore.

The present finds you better equipped to deal with what you feel you must have or do. You have gained reason and restraint in your older self and it shows. People now want to be closer to you. You no longer reek of that foul stench of collecting things. You laugh and joke and see the world for what it is and not as another ordeal you must overcome. Jörmungandr is no longer your enemy, although you are still not friends. At least you can see where your error lay.

Thor in the future over is the piece you want to have in your reading. While everyone else around you is obsessed beyond reason, you are calm and in control. You have vanquished your demons and can now see the truth behind all the theories. Some of your friends believe in aliens, lizard people living in the middle of the earth, chem trails that cause cancer, cell phones that cause cancer, water that causes cancer, but you—yes, you—know the truth to all of this. And even though you could tell them it would do no good, so you are content to listen to their foolishness, smile, and keep your own counsel.

Now, they may all be correct. All these things may indeed be real, but they don't need to involve you. You no longer need to be a part of these groups, and your obsessions that kept you up at night for years are now just dinner jokes to humor your guests. Rest knowing you are in a good place and the world would love to be where you are, just as soon as they can figure out how.

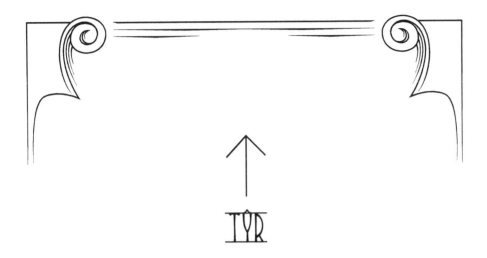

TÝR

Týr is the representative of justice and fairness, which I have always thought was incredibly foolish because he is the ultimate liar. Týr is the son of the giant Hymer, so he is in reality not an Æsir even though most people call him a god. Týr is represented with one arm due to his conflict with Fenrir.

When Fenrir was born, the gods took the great wolf to Asgard to keep an eye on him since he grew daily and they knew he would be instrumental at Ragnarök. As I wrote in the Fenrir chapter, Týr offered his hand to the wolf to guarantee that the gods would release him if he could not break the rope Gleipnir. However, Týr lied and the wolf stayed leashed. This is why I find it interesting that Týr is held up as the most honest and fair god even though he lied and cheated to gain the upper "paw" on Fenrir.

Vert

Other than the above incident, though, Týr is an upright and honest god. He travels with Thor when Thor attempts to capture Jörmungandr but is foiled by Hymer, Týr's father.

Fairness and justice are why you follow Týr. You are an honest person, and you try to do all things aboveboard and in plain sight. In your past you have excelled at this, and those who have known you or have had dealings with you have come to trust you and all that you stand for. Be proud of that. There is much deceit in the world and you will have none of it.

In the present, though, you have been a little less fair and just. You have played fast and loose with the truth at times but only for the best and purest of reasons. As Týr lied once to Fenrir for the sake of the gods and the peace of the realms, you, too, have been known to stretch the truth at times, but those times have been few and far between. And they have been for noble reasons. For that, you should be of good mind when thinking of doing it again, if you must.

Future Týr vert gives you the opportunity to help others channel their inner Týr. You are the pillar of trust and truth, but those around you need a little push. You are the push they need and you are there to give it. You know who they are and you know what you need to do, even though you may not recognize it yet. When the time comes the energy will be there and you will assist them in their goals fairly and honestly. It's a fine duty you perform and one you should and will be proud of.

Inverted

Honesty notwithstanding, Týr is known for an incredible sacrifice. He knowingly allowed Fenrir to take his right hand and part of his arm to bind the great wolf. And he did it with such a degree of calmness that even though the wolf suspected a trick, he was tricked nonetheless.

Sacrifice is something you know very well. In the past you have lost much in the name of fairness and honesty. There is a line in the sand that you will not cross, and in refusing to cross that line you have suffered. That does not mean it was in vain. The sacrifices you have made have been for the common good and, like Týr, you and the world are better for it.

The present gives you the knowledge to know what the sacrifice you are being asked to give is worth. Týr knew well enough that he would lose his arm to the jaws of the great wolf and you are no exception. You know that the situation you are in the middle of will cost you dearly, but you will go through with it anyway because it is the correct thing to do. In the end the pain will abate and you will be better for the experience even though at the moment you feel as though it's the greatest expense of your life—and it might be, but that's for another time.

Týr future will find you in the middle of a sacrifice of great proportion. The time is not yet Ragnarök, but it will seem that way to you. The disaster that is about to befall you will be great and lasting. With this warning you now have the ability to negate some of the loss and shorten the suffering. Even though the sacrifice will still occur, with planning and commitment you will come through it less scathed.

Over

As I said earlier, Týr lied. He lied so convincingly that Fenrir allowed himself to be bound for all time until Ragnarök. The deceit was complete, and even though it cost Týr his right hand and arm, the destruction of the realms was postponed.

In your past Týr inverted has given you the gift of sight. You can see through others' deceptions and avoided the traps that mere mortals have fallen into. In this age of scams, you are never tricked and your example to others is noteworthy. Great things you have done with this gift and you have saved countless others from the loss.

The present, though, is another story. You have been unable to help your friends and they have been taken advantage of. Even though you are immune to others' schemes and guile, they are not, and even now they are being abused by shysters and con artists who want their hard-earned money. Never stop trying to help them, though. They are your friends, and even if you see those who are not friends getting ready to suffer, you must assist them also. It's your lot in life to be there for those who cannot defend themselves.

In the future everyone will see the deceit of the world. You have been a credit to yourself and your gods and Týr is proud of you. All those whom you have reached out and touched are now able to see through the guile around them. Be satisfied that you will be doing a great service and everyone will profit from it—well, not everyone. Those who take advantage of the weak and the innocent shall suffer, but they deserve to and there is a special place in Helheim for them.

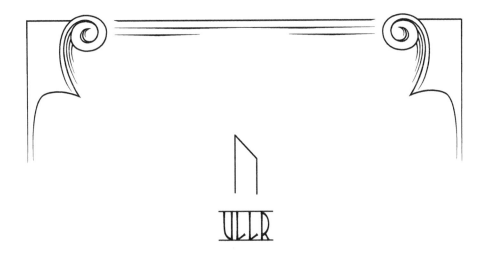

ULLR

Ullr is the god of the hunt and all that is outdoors—such as ice and snow activities—and is an exceptional archer and hunter. He is therefore prayed to by hunters, trackers, skiers, skaters, and those who spend time in the woods and mountains for their livelihood. Ullr is the son of Sif and an unknown father.

Vert

One of the traits of a hunter is persistence. Another is the pursuit of the prize, be it animal or human. In the vert position Ullr exemplifies the dogged pursuit and persistence of the hunter amidst overwhelming obstacles.

With Ullr in your past, you have shown your dedication to the hunt and the chase. You are dedicated to your craft and you show it in whatever you do. Remember, a hunt is not always physical, nor is it always for an actual trophy. In your case you have had many ephemeral chases that have taxed you and left you worn but better for the experience. These are lessons that all hunters must learn in order to improve.

Ullr in the present is your reasoning abilities. A good hunter can sniff out a trail and then, once the trail is set, sense where the prey will go next. You are learning these skills now and they will be well-utilized in your near future, so practice them with as much zeal as you can muster. If you learn your lessons now it will save you from having to relearn them later.

A famous detective was fond of saying, "the game's afoot." And in the future your game will definitely be afoot. Many have failed to track down and capture what you are now looking for, but only you will have the ability to see all the signs on the trails and trap the prize. Now, you are going to have to figure out what that prize is first since there will be more than one target of your interest, and all your interests will be of a physical and fleeting nature. Choose well, for if you choose poorly, you will regret that choice for quite some time.

Inverted

Most of us work hard. Even in the best of times we take few vacations and put in long, arduous hours at work. I retired three years ago along with a few friends I had at work and we all work just as hard and we're retired. Go figure, right? But there is a balance to work and that other side is play. You *must* learn to play as hard as you work, or the balance will be off and you will feel it in your health, head, and heart. Learn to take long walks, nap more, laugh often, and relax. Remember, a hike is a quest if you think of it that way but a hike can also just be a pleasant walk in the countryside. The choice has always been up to you.

You have been driven to work hard and play little in your past. It has gotten you to great heights and also to unbelievable lows. Your health has suffered at times and relationships have been hard at best. I'd like to say it's all been worth it, but I won't lie to you. You could have accomplished just as much if you stopped from time to time to smell the roses, watch a bird fly, or play with a puppy. It's the little things that make the difference to humans, and we as humans need these diversions or we lose sight of what is really important. As you come into your present, it's time to regain that sight.

In the present Ullr is telling you to balance your two worlds. There is a meme on social media that suggests that inside us there are two wolves. One is dark and one is light, or something like that. The meme goes on to say that the one you feed is the one that dominates your personality. I have always thought that was a stupid meme. Feed both of them equally and treat them both with respect. In life you need both light and dark as well as you need work and play. You cannot have one without the other and now is the time to realize that and utilize that knowledge.

Congratulations. You have finally learned your lessons. In the future you will know when to work and when to play. You will understand that Asgard and Helheim are two sides of the same coin and it depends on which side you get when you flip the coin. However, you will also learn that there are benefits to both realms, and as you learn this you will understand how to use them to your advantage. Odin and Hel both have things to teach us. Work hard to learn those things and then play hard with them.

Over

We all want a better place. Some of us see that place as a farm, the lake, the ocean, the mountains, another country—the list is endless. Ullr sees his better place as the forest and who can fault him for that? The cool of the mornings with dew-soaked underbrush. Birds singing in the trees and game plentiful in the brush. If that is your idea of a better place, then this piece is for you.

Your past has been spent looking for that better place. Unfortunately, nothing and nowhere you have gone has given you that peace of mind that you so desperately needed and wanted. That doesn't mean it's not out there; it just means that you haven't found it yet. As you look back on the past, you can now see where you missed clues and made mistakes. There were hints aplenty to finding this secret garden that would so invigorate you, but you were too busy with the hunt to see the prize. Now that it's in the past, maybe you can take some time and look again at the clues. They're still there. You just have to look harder.

The present Ullr over is one of discovery. As you go through your day-to-day routine, you are coming closer to that better place. You just haven't quite put your finger on the location yet. Others seem to have found theirs and left to live that special life, leaving you feeling alone. It's not personal, really. You have just taken more time than they did. And it will take more time still because you are too caught up in the small shiny things to see the grand prize.

It won't be until your future that your special and better place will reveal itself. After a lifetime of searching, it's finally time to settle down and escape to a better place. You have worked hard and long for this and deserve all you get. And whatever the prize is, remember, it's your prize. It may not be exactly what you thought you wanted, or it may be exactly what you didn't want, but it's what the Norns have said you needed and deserved, and this time there is no changing fate. And in the end, that's all this is about, right? Fate.

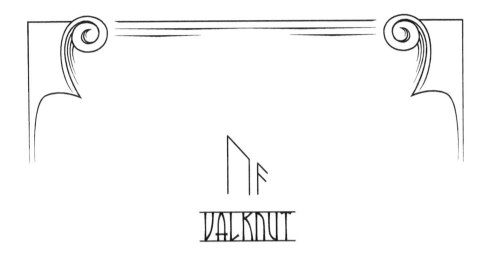

VALKNUT

The Valknut is often associated with Odin but there is no indication that this is true. The symbol is three interlocking triangles. There are examples of the Valknut carved on ship burials and it could be a symbol of the dead, but again that is supposition. Another idea is that the symbol represents the nine realms since there are nine sides to the three triangles.

There are two different designs that appear with this symbol. One is a continuous band that makes the three triangles without distinctive separations. The second symbol is the three distinct triangles that are interconnected. Either way, this symbol is one of the major ones that represent modern Heathenism, for better or for worse. You will see this symbol on shields, boxes, stones, and other decorations.

Vert

The Valknut is sort of like a Möbius strip; at least, one of the types is. The three triangles are interconnected and that's exactly what the Valknut represents in the vert position. Everything is connected to everything is connected … you get the idea, right?

In your past you have had connections that have worked, connections that haven't, and connections that weren't even close enough to warrant being called connections. Think about all of them. What did they all have in common? You, that's what. You are the connecting pin that joins everything in your universe. But that makes sense because it is, after all, your universe. While, according to the game, actor Kevin Bacon may have six degrees of separation, you can claim one. Everything is connected to you. Think about that as you look back on your past and what you have and haven't accomplished. This is a time of introspection.

Your present, though, is about as different from your past as you can get. With the Valknut in vert present, every connection is a missed one. You just can't seem to get it right. The problem is you. Slow down and take the time to work out the details of the connections. Just because they worked for you in the past doesn't mean they're going to work for you now. Work on your game plan.

In the future you will finally figure everything out. If you need to borrow something, you'll know who to call. Need to get a deal on something you can't afford? You got this. People want a party but don't know who to call? You do. Everything will fit together and you will enjoy amazing productivity and acclaim. It's about time, don't you think?

Inverted

The Valknut is a great symbol of power, but it is also one of memorialization. Gravestones, monuments, and burials are all examples of the Valknut protecting the dead as they travel to Valhalla.

This piece in the past is your connection to your ancestors. They are who made you and who influenced you. If you remember those who came before you, then you are lucky. If you cannot remember those who bore and sired you, remember they were of great stock because you are an incredible individual. We are all a combination of our past memories and experiences. Anytime you need clarity, look to those who came before you and know that you are watched, loved, and protected.

In the present the inverted Valknut will calm you. There is great anxiety about death and dying. Few of us are content with the knowledge that we will either go to Valhalla, Folkvang, or Helheim. For that reason we block out those thoughts and look for other religions that offer a more promising afterlife. Do not be fooled, though, by these other paths. Stay your course and you will drink and fight with the Æsir in the golden hall of Odin. This is your test. Do not fail it.

The Valknut is not about dying. It is about the dead and their purpose at Ragnarök. As you look to your future and your mortality, remember that everything dies on this realm, but we never really die in the eye of Odin. We are just moved from one place to another. And in that other place, even though to get there takes the ultimate sacrifice and loss, the destination is worth all that you must pass through. Death is inevitable. Look to it as an old friend with whom you have been corresponding all your life. And with that thought, be at peace.

Over

The Valknut is power. Make no mistake about the sheer power that this symbol generates. Go to any gathering and you will see the Valknut on shields, mugs, tents, clothing, and furniture. Those who follow this symbol have given it the position it deserves in the modern Heathen movement and, as our ancestors showed in carvings, the symbol will lead us through.

Your past has been without focus. As you look back you can easily see how you strayed from your path and sought guidance in other lights. None of them worked for you and now you are back to your Heathen roots and under the power of the Valknut. Do not fool yourself, though; this is just a symbol, nothing more. There is no mystical power behind it that you do not give it. The real power was in you all along, you just needed to understand that, and now as you look back you can see all the areas where you failed to grasp that simple fact. At least now you know, and you shall take that knowledge with you.

Sitting now in the present you are without the power you crave. This piece is your warning that power is not always what it should be. The character of

Ragnar Lothbrok in the *Vikings* television series says it best: "Power is always dangerous. It attracts the worst and corrupts the best. Power is only given to those who are prepared to lower themselves to pick it up."[45] While a little power is essential in everyone's life, excessive or absolute power is fatal to the soul. Lower your expectations and your ambitions. With absolute power comes absolute responsibility, and that takes its toll on the body and the mind.

Your future Valknut over never comes. You will spend your entire life chasing the power that will always elude you. Accept that now. Be content with what you have and all the advantages you have been offered in this world and accept that utter and total power is something you will never accomplish. There are far better things in this world than being powerful. Strive to be loved, respected, and admired. The powerful are often envied, hated, and feared.

---

45. *Vikings*, season 3, episode 1, "Mercenary," directed by Ken Girotti, written by Michael Hirst, featuring Travis Fimmel, Katheryn Winnick, Clive Standen, aired February 19, 2015, on the History Channel.

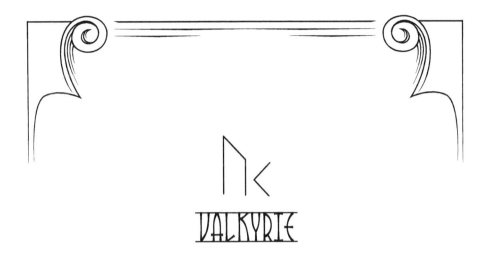

ᚾ< VALKYRIE

While the Valkyries are portrayed as beautiful armored women riding winged horses, the truth is pretty close to that. These women are representatives of Odin to a degree. However, they are also independent agents on the battlefield. They have swayed one side or the other depending on their wont, and they have the power to pick and choose whom they believe are worthy of Valhalla or Folkvang.

The Valkyries are fierce maidens in armor and helm that carry shield and spear and ride rightly on powerful steeds. They have names such as Skögul and Göndul, Gunnr and Hildr, Hjörþrimul and Geirskögul.[46] When not watching over battles, these warrior women serve the dead mead in Valhalla as the warriors feast each night.

Valkyries have no preference for either side. They will take both sides in battles and wander through the fighting to see who is worthy of Valhalla and who is not. If they see someone they think should go to the halls of the dead,

---

46. Seigfried, ed., *The Illustrated Völuspá*, 60.

they take them up on their steed and ride away with them to the great halls, where the dead will fight and feast until Ragnarök.

Vert

With the Valkyries, it's all about being worthy. Not the "I'm not worthy of Mjölnir" kind of worthy but the "worthy of going to Valhalla" kind of worthy. Remember, though, that it's not just on the battlefield where worthiness is tested, even though that's where you get to prove your mettle. You must also be worthy as a person. Do you honor your gods? Do you honor your king and your country? Finally, do you honor yourself? These are questions we should ask ourselves every day, even now.

In the past you failed to ask yourself these questions enough. You are worthy, but you doubt yourself and your ability. Even though others proclaim that you are an upright and honorable person, you personally keep yourself from reaching your full potential. Look hard at who you are and how long you have been that way. You will see that you are finer than you give yourself credit for. It's time to level up and take that next step to greatness.

Present Valkyrie vert has others questioning your worthiness. You know you are worthy and everything you have done is aboveboard and honorable, but there are those out there who are jealous of you and sow seeds of doubt about you. There is nothing you can do to dissuade these people from detracting from you, and if you try it will only look worse for you. Therefore, you need to keep your head up, your heart pure, and your spirit clean. Those who matter will see through the subterfuge and recognize the truth. The rest are not worthy of your time.

In the future you will be called upon to assist someone else in their quest for worthiness. You know how hard it was for you and you see the struggle they are going through. Take the time to offer a hand and advice. Help is a free gift that never needs to be repaid and advice may be what it takes to turn their life around. When you help others you inadvertently help yourself.

Inverted

Many of us think that death is the end and once you die there is nothing left. The Valkyries know the truth, that death is just another transition and you are leaving everything behind and starting over. Do not fear death. It's an old friend who walks with you every day. Its twin is life and the two keep you balanced. If you pay too much attention to one and not the other, you will become scattered and ineffective. Only when you understand that without life there can be no death, and without death there is no balance to your life, will you know true joy and happiness. Oh, and become worthy. You knew I was going to say that, didn't you?

The past has seen you struggle with death. People you have known, your family and friends have passed away, leaving you behind. You feel guilt about what you might have said before they died or what you might have done, but the dead no longer care. There is nothing you can do or say that will affect them. They have gone on to another adventure and you are the one that must deal with it. Trust me when I say that the dead are happier than the living in many instances. It may be difficult to believe but it's the truth nonetheless.

In the present there is nothing left for you. You are having a hard time dealing with the world around you and you feel that you no longer wish to suffer the day-to-day occurrences. You may even have thought about joining the dead. Don't do it. Suicide is no honorable way to die. You are feeling dejected and, dare I say it, unworthy. As a mental health professional with a masters in counselor education and as a member of the National Board for Certified Counselors, I cannot stress enough that even though that end seems optimal, the long-term ramifications are dire. Suffer if you must. Pay a heavy price if you must. But stay and fight the good fight until your time comes naturally. If you are struggling with suicidal thoughts, there are many help lines that can help and will be of service. Reach out to any of them if you feel the need and protect yourself. Please.

The future finds you thinking about your own mortality. You feel as though you haven't done enough in your life and you long to do more. If that is the way you feel, then do something about it. I know so many people who waste their lives wanting to do more but fail to because they just get waylaid by externalities. Leave a legacy. It's the greatest thing you can do in your life. Paint, write, teach, build—whatever you wish to do, you need to do it. As you get older your time gets closer to that last breath and only the Norns know when that is. Every day when you awake is another chance to make a difference. You don't have to die to start over. You can start over every new day.

Over

Over and inverted with the Valkyries are very similar. While the inverted is about starting over, the over is about going to a better situation. While they may look similar, they are not always. Valkyrie over is about moving on and moving up. The Valkyries took the honored dead in battle and lofted them to a status of almost gods. They fought all day and then drank and feasted all night. Their lives were much improved after their deaths.

In the past the world was a better place to be. As they say, hindsight is twenty-twenty. You look back at the past and think that it was everything you could have imagined. You long for the good old days. Wake up! There were no good old days. Every day we move forward in our evolution, our world gets better, even though you might not believe that. There have always been wars, famines, pestilence, and disasters. In twenty years, today will be the good old days, so it's time to put this fallacy to bed and turn it around 180 degrees. Your past was a prelude to a better situation in the future, which is now your present. Once you can see that, you can move forward and make every day even more important.

Speaking of the present, it's here. You are still looking for a better situation, but at least you have a clue what that situation looks like. And you think you know how to get there. That's two out of the three necessities for a bright future. All you need now is the future to arrive. Unfortunately, it won't for a while, so live in the present. Make your situation better now. Go out and meet people. Help your neighbors. Grow vegetables. Adopt a stray animal. Volunteer at a shelter or become a tutor. Remember, everyone else is looking for a better situation too. What you do will create that situation for someone else and they in turn will create it for you.

As we age, we look back and think of what we did and what we didn't do. Many of us long for our youth or a lost love. Back then, we never thought we'd be old enough to think about death, but here it is. And telling yourself you're going to a better situation after you die doesn't seem to help all that much. So what's the alternative? I have said it before: leave a legacy! A better situation may be a metaphor. It may be a dream. But a legacy is real. It's tangible in the ethereal. You can never undo a legacy. And in that respect, your legacy will give others the better situation they want to go to.

YGGDRASIL

It's hard to say anything new on Yggdrasil this far into the book. I have talked about the roots drawing water from the three wells. I've given the names and species of the animals that live under, over, and in the great ash tree, and after Ragnarök how it again connects the nine realms.

Suffice it to say that the tree is essential to the cosmology of the Norse and their pantheon. Without the tree, mankind would eventually die out at Ragnarök, for it is Yggdrasil where Líf and Lífþrasir, man and woman, are safely protected until they emerge again to repopulate Midgard.[47] Odin would not have gained the runes and mastery of seiðr. There would be nothing to connect the nine realms in the universe, and, finally, there would be no place for Ratatoskr to run up and down chasing eagles and serpents just to irk them.

---

47. Davidson, *Gods and Myths of the Viking Age*, 202.

Vert

To say that Yggdrasil is strength is an understatement. There is nothing more powerful in the nine realms or in the cosmos than the great tree. While it was not there at the beginning, it will be there at the end and the power that it exhibits throughout the midtime has inspired sagas.

The great tree has been your tree since you were born. You may not have known it, or you may have wondered why you were drawn to the forest and to ashes in particular, but the tree has watched over you since your beginning. When you needed strength you received it from Yggdrasil. You dreamed of this great ash and it comforted you in your times of need. Be of strong conviction in all things you do, and the great ash will be there to assist and guide you. Even now, in the present, if you need help or inspiration, look to Yggdrasil.

Yggdrasil in the present is a warning of what you need *now*. You are about to embark on a journey that will take you into great danger and wonder. To prepare you for this, you need a piece of the great tree, even if it's a representation of the actual Yggdrasil. Go to the forest, the trees, or a lumber yard. Find a piece of ash. Fashion a wand from it in whatever shape you determine is best for you and carry it with you. Draw strength from this talisman and you will vanquish all that stand against you.

Far in the future the ash will be there at the end. Yggdrasil in the future is the knowledge that you will someday see the great tree again. Take solace from the fact that as you near your final days and hours, Odin shall present you with the opportunity to visit the ash one last time.

Inverted

Everything is connected by Yggdrasil. The nine realms are accessible from the branches of the great ash. Knowledge, seiðr, and even magic may be found in its branches along with a myriad of animals great and small.

As I have said a couple of times in this book, everything is connected to everything is connected to everything is … With Yggdrasil inverted in your past you have experienced those connections. Through the branches of the great tree you have made many friends, some enemies, and accomplished great and minor things. Without these connections you would be nothing, so be thankful for them all, even the ones that didn't turn out too well (you know the one I'm talking about). Continue making these connections and you will continue to prosper and thrive. Cut these ties and so will your fortunes be cut and winnowed.

The present Yggdrasil inverted is a lot more than a few connections at a bar or meeting room. You need to get out into the streets and make the hard connections. There are people that you need to meet and get to know who don't know you exist. Without them your life could be a lot darker and poorer. You might not even know who they are yet, but you need to connect with them.

How do you do that? Good question. Here's a suggestion: Find those in your network that know some of what you need. Then ask them to connect you with their mentors and teachers. If you don't get what you want from these secondary folks, ask them for *their* mentors, and on and on. Don't give up, and keep at it until you find those who will get you where you need to go.

In the future you will be cutting ties. You have made so many connections that many are redundant. While a small cadre is essential in any relationship, an assembly of hundreds is just too unmanageable. Cull your lists and you will find that your peace and prosperity will increase manyfold. A warning on this, though. When you cut your ties, do it with grace and appreciation. Some of these will be necessary again and you don't want to alienate anyone as you thin your herd.

Over

After Ragnarök, Yggdrasil will be the safe haven of Líf and Lífþrasir. These two will emerge to repopulate the human race. It will be a time of rebirth and renewal and the great ash will be there still.

In your past you have had some rebirth of your own. You have rebranded yourself and started over again. Whether you were successful or not is up to you and you alone, but the fact that you took the plunge and the risk speaks volumes about you. Stand by your choices, and no matter who or what tries to dissuade you from those choices, you must turn your back on them. You made the right decision. Be strong with that.

In the present, though, you are going to be presented with more challenges to change. Look hard at the options and feel free to walk away. Not all rebirth and renewal are warranted, and in this day and age, sometimes it's best to stay with the safe and known over the uncertain and risky.

Everything will balance out in your future. All the changes you went through and the ones you turned down will come to pass and you will be whole and complete—not always the same thing. Be of good mind that your future self will be well-adjusted and settled. All the decisions you made and followed through on are now over, and the results are stunning.

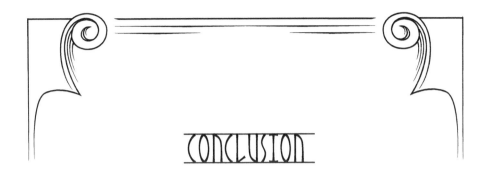

CONCLUSION

The old woman looked at the three bearded men sitting in her hut and picked up a small leather bag. The hut was cramped with the four sitting around the fire since the hut usually only housed the old woman, who was frail and small. She turned out the contents of the leather bag onto a worn blanket and stared for some time in the firelight.

"You will have a harsh winter," she began. "Plan now for more snow and ice than ever before. And just before you think you are out of everything in your larder, the winter will end and all will be plentiful." She looked at the man farthest from her. He was younger than the other two and had not yet seen his first raid.

"Terrik, you will sail west this spring and not return." She saw the young man drop his eyes and then raise them in shock. She then continued, "You will find what you are looking for in the west and stay there." The younger man looked relieved.

After telling each their fate in the upcoming spring raids, the old woman dismissed the three. "I am tired and you have what you seek," she said. "You may pay at the door."

The three men rose and as they left the hut each left a large cod in a wooden bucket. It was their payment for a reading of their fate.

Did this ever happen? Probably not exactly the way portrayed here but something similar did at least a thousand times over the course of the Norse expansion. Sailors, farmers, travelers, pregnant women, all came to the seers for readings and paid with produce. It was the way of the Norse. And in that reading you see how essential divination was and remains.

Throughout this book I have talked about the past, the present, and the future. The past is everything you have ever experienced right up to the very point that you are living now. Each second you live, your past increases and your future decreases. The only thing that remains constant is the present. The present never changes in time. It is the exact instance that you exist in now. In most if not all of the chapters I have mentioned the future as though you can reach it. What you actually reach is the far present, but the future is what we are used to saying. It's complicated and I have yet to figure out a better way to explain it. Suffice it to say that the future is far away. You will someday think you have reached it, but what you will have actually done is gotten to a later present. Bottom line is, don't worry about it. Think of the future as what is to come. After all, past, present, and future are just place-holders. Before humanity started using those terms, they probably used others. The names may change but the concept never does.

After I finished writing this, I reread it about a dozen times. Each time I realized more and more that this book is as much philosophy as it is history and divination. There is a world out there that we all think we understand but we really don't. We try to get a grip on who we are and what we are about by dreaming, writing, and even fortune-telling. Through the centuries there have been tea leaves in cups, I Ching rods used by Chinese masters, horoscopes, and astrology. The tarot industry is a billion dollar one and there are more and more new decks being produced every year. And of course there are the rune stones.

And now there is this book. It's different but also similar to all the rest of the divination tools. You take what you already know, apply it to a decision, allow the gods to lead you into choosing the answers that you may or may not want, and then try to ascertain what they are telling you.

You now know everything I do about the gods and how to divinate. I've tried to give you an enjoyable read while teaching you my world and my gods as I see them. If I have, then I've succeeded. If I've failed, then that's on me. Either way, I wish you great renown in all the presents that have yet to be since, as I said earlier, the present is all you ever get and the future never really comes.

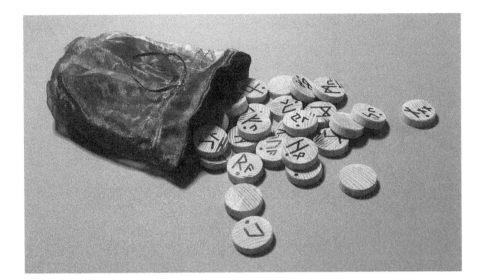

Part 3

ADDITIONAL ENTITIES

I have included these additional pieces because in their own rights they have a place in the cosmology of the Norse pantheon. They are, though, not pieces that I have worked with as much as the others and I am still ironing out the kinks, so to speak. However, I feel that many of you may wish to add these to your divination bag, so I include them here. This is what I know of them and what they have said to me so far.

Angrboða

Angrboða is the mother of monsters. With Loki she had the great wolf Fenrir, the Midgard Serpent Jörmungandr, and the goddess Hel.[48] These three creatures will be instrumental at Ragnarök and, with their father, Loki, and the giants of Jotunheim and Muspelheim, shall destroy Midgard and Asgard, laying these realms to burning ash and waste.

Auðhumla

Auðhumla is the great cosmic cow that licked the salt from the frost between Muspelheim and Niflheim to expose Buri. The sagas state that Auðhumla also nourished the giant Ymir from her teats and was eventually washed over the edge of the cosmos by the blood deluge of Odin, Vili, and Ve as they killed Ymir.[49]

Draupnir

Draupnir is the ring created by the dwarf brothers Sindri and Brokkr. This golden ring, given to Odin, replicates itself eight times every ninth night. The replicated rings are all exact copies of the original.

---

48. Taylor, ed., *Norse Myths & Tales: Anthology of Classic Tales*, 62–64.

49. Lindow, *Norse Mythology*, 63.

Hoenir

Hoenir is a friend of Odin's as well as the cause of Mimir losing his head. As I mentioned earlier, without Mimir, Hoenir was unable to make decisions or render suitable solutions to the Vanir's questions. When they discovered the ruse, they beheaded Mimir instead of Hoenir. After Ragnarök, Hoenir will be there with the survivors to repopulate new Asgard.[50]

Sjöfn

Very little is known about Sjöfn. She is the goddess of love, lust, and marriage. She is also given credit for being able to influence both men and women in the ways of love and marriage. This makes her a powerful goddess, if that is true. However, she may also be a kenning for Frigg since the All Mother is capable of doing the same things. Either way, Sjöfn is related to the marriage bed and marriage rights and is honored for those abilities.

Snotra

Very little is known of Snotra. She is the goddess of wisdom and one of Frigg's handmaidens. Other than that, she is not mentioned.

---

50. Seigfried, ed., *The Illustrated Völuspá*, 115.

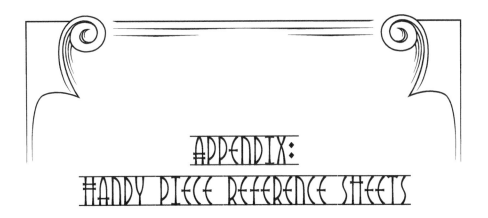

APPENDIX:
HANDY PIECE REFERENCE SHEETS

Angrboða	Vert	A mother's love at all costs
	Inverted	Bringing sorrow and harm through actions
	Over	Being blamed for what you do
Auðhumla	Vert	Giving nourishment and life
	Inverted	Freeing the captured or enslaved
	Over	Opportunities lost
Baldr	Vert	Beauty, love, acceptance
	Inverted	Sacrifice
	Over	Betrayal, secrecy, jealousy
Bifröst	Vert	Connections
	Inverted	Lost connections
	Over	Disconnections

Bragi	Vert	Entertained, informed
	Inverted	Welcoming, dealing with the dead
	Over	Misrepresented, misled, misinformed
Draupnir	Vert	An original, not a copy or an imitation
	Inverted	To create endlessly and to perfection
	Over	Do not lose your head over what you cannot control
Fenrir	Vert	Destruction
	Inverted	Darkness
	Over	Resentment, distrust
Freyja	Vert	Chief of the Valkyries, honor in death
	Inverted	Love and beauty
	Over	Carnal knowledge
Freyjr	Vert	Growing, expanding
	Inverted	Contracting
	Over	Winter, cold, desolate
Frigg	Vert	All Mother
	Inverted	Home mother
	Over	Vengeful matriarch
Fulla	Vert	Helpful, assisting, caring
	Inverted	Secretive
	Over	Healing of animals
Gjallarhorn	Vert	Warning
	Inverted	Preparation
	Over	Too late, the giants are already at the door

Heimdallur	Vert	Guardian
	Inverted	All-seeing, all-knowing
	Over	End of things
Hel	Vert	Queen of Helheim
	Inverted	Rebirth and restart
	Over	Search deep for decisions
Höðr	Vert	Blind to what is actually happening
	Inverted	Being led somewhere you shouldn't go
	Over	Too trusting and gullible
Hoenir	Vert	Misinterpreted
	Inverted	A survivor, one who wins over adversity
	Over	A steady helper, a friend to the end
Huginn	Vert	Clear vision
	Inverted	Confusion
	Over	Observation and information
Iðunn	Vert	Immortality
	Inverted	Sickness and death
	Over	Health and caring
Jörmungandr	Vert	Status quo, all is in balance
	Inverted	Refusal to let go, holding on
	Over	Dire consequences, destruction is imminent
Loki	Vert	Deceit, trickery
	Inverted	Selfishness
	Over	Forced assistance

Mimisbrunnr	Vert	Blamed for others' failures
	Inverted	Guardian of secrets and wisdom
	Over	Wise council

Mistletoe	Vert	Insignificance, overlooked as not worthy
	Inverted	Taken advantage of, used against your will
	Over	Death of beauty

Mjölnir	Vert	Power
	Inverted	Defense
	Over	Worthiness

Muninn	Vert	Things remembered
	Inverted	Things forgotten
	Over	Being relied upon, being dependable

Nanna	Vert	Everything for love
	Inverted	Sacrifice for another
	Over	True love at any cost

Niðhöggr	Vert	Erosion, constant destruction
	Inverted	Eternal duty
	Over	Anchoring

Njörðr	Vert	Making choices unconventionally
	Inverted	Honoring one's promise
	Over	Taking nothing too seriously

The Norns	Vert	Urðr, the Crone, the past is inescapable
	Inverted	Verðandi, the Mother, nurturing in the present
	Over	Skuld, the Maiden, innocence, the future never arrives

Odin	Vert	The All Father, ruler of all things
	Inverted	Insatiable thirst for wisdom
	Over	The creator and destroyer
Ragnarök	Vert	Destruction
	Inverted	Starting over
	Over	Everything is already known
Ratatoskr	Vert	Messenger
	Inverted	Instigator
	Over	Chaos
Sif	Vert	Harvest and plenty
	Inverted	Preparation
	Over	Barrenness
Sjofn	Vert	Love
	Inverted	Marriage
	Over	Love or marriage gone awry
Sleipnir	Vert	Travel away
	Inverted	Travel back, return from a journey
	Over	Strength in battle, winning over insurmountable odds
Snotra	Vert	Assistance to others
	Inverted	Great wisdom is not beyond your capabilities
	Over	With wisdom comes responsibility
Surtr	Vert	The creator, the one who is first, there at the beginning
	Inverted	Ancient knowledge, knowing things of old
	Over	The destroyer, one who ends everything

Thor	Vert	Great power for goodness
	Inverted	Quick to anger, quick to react, quick to fight
	Over	Obsessed beyond reason
Tyr	Vert	Fairness, justice
	Inverted	Sacrifice
	Over	Deceit
Ullr	Vert	Dogged pursuit
	Inverted	Playing as hard as you work
	Over	Escape to a better place
Valknut	Vert	Interconnectivity
	Inverted	The dead but not dying
	Over	Power
Valkyrie	Vert	Worthiness
	Inverted	Leaving all behind, starting over
	Over	Going to a better situation
Yggdrasil	Vert	Strength
	Inverted	Connection
	Over	Rebirth, renewal

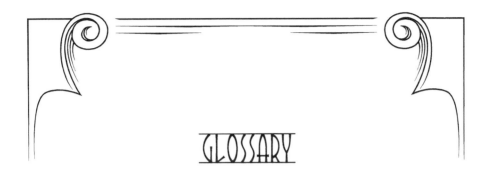

GLOSSARY

Alfheim: place, home of the light elves. See Freyjr in chapters. See realms.

Alfrik: person, dwarf. One of the four dwarves that spent the night with Freyja for her to gain Brísingamen.

All Father: person, god, another name for Odin.

All Mother: person, god, another name for Frigg.

Angrboða: person, giant. Mother of Hel, Fenrir, and Jörmungandr with Loki.

apples: thing, see fruit.

Asgard: place, the home and realm of the gods and goddesses. Home to the Æsir and those others who are fortunate enough to be there. To reach Asgard from Midgard you must cross Bifröst, the rainbow bridge, watched over by Heimdallur.

Aurboða: person, giant. Wife of Gymir and mother of Gerðr and Beli.

Auðhumla: animal, cosmic cow. The second creature to emerge from the ice at the creation of the cosmos. Auðhumla nourished Ymir with milk from her udders and in turn was nourished from salt in the great ice of space. She is responsible for licking Buri from the ice.

Austur: direction. Icelandic for *east*.

Austri: person, dwarf. The dwarf that holds up the eastern corner of the skull of Ymir, creating the sky.

Baldr: person, god. Son of Odin and Frigg. Most beautiful of all the gods. Killed by his brother Höðr during a trick by Loki. See Baldr in chapters.

Balderus: person, human. Another name for Baldr. See Baldr in chapters.

Baugi: person, giant. Brother of Suttung. Odin enlisted Baugi's help in retrieving the mead of poetry. See Odin in chapters.

Beli: person, giant. Brother of Gerðr. Son of Gymir and Aurboða.

Bergelmir: person, giant. The only male giant to survive the murder of Ymir. He and his wife (who is not named) escaped with a makeshift boat to Niflheim, where they created a race of ice giants.

Berling: person, dwarf. One of the four dwarves who spent the night with Freyja for her to gain Brísingamen.

Bestla: person, giant. With Bor, the mother of Odin, Vili, and Ve.

Bifröst: thing, the rainbow bridge that connects Midgard to Asgard. See Bifröst in chapters.

Blot: thing, ritual. A ritual at a specific time of the year, usually considered the equinoxes and solstices. In medieval times the blots were a time of sacrifice to the gods or a specific god. Now the sacrifice is "usually" metaphoric.

Bor: person, god. Son of Buri. Father of Odin, Vili, and Ve.

Bölverkr: person, god. Another name for Odin. See Odin in chapters.

Bragi: person, god. God of poetry and entertainment. See Bragi in chapters.

Brísingamen: thing, the necklace that Freyja just had to possess at the expense of her sexual purity. See Brísingamen in chapters.

Buri: person, god. Buri was the first of the Æsir to be released from the great ice flow at the creation of the realms. Buri has a son, Bor, who with his wife, the giant Bestla, has three children: Odin, Vili, and Ve.

Dag: person, giant. Son of Nat. He drives the chariot that brings day to the world.

Draupnir: thing, a ring made by two dwarves for Odin that would reproduce itself eightfold every nine nights.

Dáinn: animal, deer. One of the four deer that graze in the branches of Yggdrasil and chew the leaves and buds.

Duneyrr: animal, deer. One of the four deer that graze in the branches of Yggdrasil and chew the leaves and buds.

Duraþrór: animal, deer. One of the four deer that graze in the branches of Yggdrasil and chew the leaves and buds.

Dvalinn: animal, deer. One of the four deer that graze in the branches of Yggdrasil and chew the leaves and buds.

Dvalinn: person, dwarf. One of the four dwarves who spent the night with Freyja for her to gain Brísingamen.

eagle: animal, unnamed. The great unnamed eagle that sits at the top of Yggdrasil and listens as Ratatoskr insults it daily.

Eikthyrinir: animal, stag. The stag that lives atop Valhalla and eats of the leaves of Yggdrasil. The mist from the tree forms droplets on his horns and these drops of water feed the stream at Hvergelmir.

einherjar: person, human or god. Those who fight and die. Those who are brought to either Folkvang or Valhalla after an honorable death.

Eldjotnar: person, giant. Fire giants that live in Muspelheim.

Eriendsson, Haukr: person, human. An Icelandic lawspeaker who wrote the manuscript *Hauksbók* (the book of Hauk) that includes the *Völuspá*. A copy of the manuscript in pieces is in the Árni Magnússon Institute for Icelandic Studies in Reykjavik.

Erikson, Leifr: person, human explorer. Son of Erik the Red. Leifr is credited with being the founder of the first settlement in Greenland and discovering North America, establishing a settlement at L'Anse aux Meadows in Newfoundland.

Eyrarland farm: place, farm. A farm in the northern region of Iceland around the city of Akureyri. Around 1816 a small bronze statue was found that is thought to be Thor holding Mjölnir. The statue is dated to about 1000 CE.

Fafnir: animal, dragon. A dwarf who became a dragon to hoard the gold given to his father for the death of his brother Ötr. When Loki returned the otter skin filled with cursed gold, Fafnir killed his father and took the gold to the mountains, where he eventually turned into a dragon. Dripping venom and living in a cave, Fafnir killed anyone who ventured into his realm after his gold. He was eventually killed by Sigurd.

Fensalir: place, Frigg's hall in Asgard. See Frigg in chapters.

Fenrir: animal, the great wolf. Brother of Hel. See Fenrir in chapters.

Fjalar: person, dwarf. One of the two dwarves who killed Kvasir and brewed his blood into mead. See Odin in chapters.

Fjölsvinnsmál: thing, poem. An Old Norse poem. See Surtr in chapters.

Folkvang: place, the great hall of Freyja where half the fallen warriors worthy of Valhalla go.

forníslenzk: word. An Icelandic word meaning *Old Icelandic.* Used in relation to the sagas in contrast to Old Norse, which is now referred to as *Old Norwegian.*

Forseti: person, Æsir. Son of Baldr and Nanna.

Freki: animal, wolf. One of the two wolves that accompanies Odin when he travels through the nine realms. See Odin in chapters.

Freyjr: person, Vanir. Son of Njörðr and brother of Freyja. See Freyjr in chapters.

Freyja: person, Vanir. Daughter of Njörðr and sister of Freyjr. See Freyja in chapters.

Frigg: person, goddess. Wife of Odin. See Frigg in chapters.

Fulla: person, goddess. Handmaiden and confidant to Frigg. See Fulla in chapters.

Futhark, Elder: item. An ancient form of runic alphabet first used by the Germanic peoples of Europe during the migration period. There are twenty-four runes in the Elder Futhark corresponding roughly to letters currently used in the English language.

Futhark, Younger: item. A shortened form of the Elder Futhark used during the exploratory period of Norse expansion. There are sixteen runes in the Younger Futhark and they are more aligned to modern-day letters and usage.

Galar: person, dwarf. One of the two dwarves who killed Kvasir and brewed his blood into mead. See Odin in chapters.

Garm: animal, wolf. The wolf that kills Týr at Ragnarök. See Týr in chapters.

Geirskögul: person, Valkyrie. One of the Valkyries. See Valkyrie in chapters.

Geri: animal, wolf. One of the two wolves that accompanies Odin when he travels through the nine realms. See Odin in chapters.

Gervaris: person, human. Possibly another name for King Gewar of Norway. See Baldr in chapters.

Gerðr: person, giant. Wife of Freyjr. See Freyjr in chapters.

Gesta Danorum: thing, translated as the *Deeds of the Danes.* This is the work of Saxo Grammaticus. Along with Snorri Sturluson's work, it comprises much of what we know about the Norse pantheon.

Gilling: person, giant. He and his wife were killed by Fjalar and Galar for no particular reason. See Odin in chapters.

Ginnungagap: thing, the great void. The eternal darkness and peace at the beginning of everything that lay between Muspelheim and Niflheim. It was here that creation occurred.

Gjallarbú: thing, bridge. The bridge over the river Gjöll leading to Helheim. See Hel in chapters.

Gjallarhorn: thing, horn. The horn of Heimdallur that he will blow to warn the gods at the beginning of Ragnarök. See Gjallarhorn in chapters.

Gjöll: thing, river. The river that protects the other realms from Helheim or the other way around. Guarded by the giantess Móðguðr. See Hel in chapters.

Gleipnir: thing, rope. The rope created by the dwarves to bind the wolf Fenrir. It was made out of six impossible things: the spit of a bird, the breath of a fish, the roots of a mountain, the sound of a cat walking, the beard of a woman, and the sinews of a bear. When Fenrir breaks his restraints, he will usher in Ragnarök.

Göndul: person, Valkyrie. One of the Valkyries. See Valkyrie in chapters.

Grer: person, dwarf. One of the four dwarves that spent the night with Freyja for her to gain Brísingamen.

Grimnismál: thing, translated as the "Sayings of Grimnir." One of the poems of the *Poetic Edda* from the Codex Regius. Grimnir is one of the alternate personas of Odin.

Griðr: person, giant. Mother of Viðar with Odin.

Groa: person, witch. A magic worker who attempts to remove the piece of whetstone from the head of Thor. See Thor in chapters.

Gullfaxi: animal, horse. Horse owned by Hrungnir. Lost in a wager to Odin and given to Magni by Thor for lifting the leg of Hrungnir from his throat. See Thor in chapters.

Gullinbursti: animal, a boar created in the forges of Brokkr and Sindri. While at the forge, Brokkr threw a boar's skin into the forge and created a magical boar for Freyjr whose bristles could glow in the dark.

Gungnir: thing, spear. The spear of Odin. It never misses what it is thrown at.

Gunnlöð: person, giant. Daughter of Suttung. Tasked to protect the mead of poetry under the mountain Hnitbjorg. With Odin, the mother of Bragi. See Odin in chapters.

Gunnr: person, Valkyrie. One of the Valkyries. See Valkyries in chapters.

Gylfaginning: thing, part of Snorri's *Prose Edda* about the creation and destruction of the nine realms.

Gymir: person, giant. Wife of Aurboða, father of Gerðr and Beli, and cousin to Þjazi.

Gyðja: title, the priestess or high priestess of the Ásatrú religion still practiced in many parts of Scandinavia. The Gyðja is oftentimes paired with her male counterpart, a Goði, to lead blots and other religious celebrations.

Hati Hrodvitnisson: wolf, giant. One of two wolves to chase Sol and Mani around the world until they consume them at Ragnarök.

Hauksbók: thing, book. A handwritten manuscript in Icelandic by the law-speaker Haukr Eriendsson that includes the *Völuspá.*

Heimdallur: person, god. Guardian of Bifröst. See Heimdallur in chapters.

Hel: person, giant. Hel is the queen of the dead in Helheim. She is the daughter of two giants: Loki and Angrboða. Her siblings are Fenrir the wolf and Jörmungandr the Midgard Serpent. She will usher in Ragnarök at the end of time and see the new beginning. Often described as half hideous and half beautiful. See Hel in chapters.

Hermoðr: person, god. Lives in Asgard. We only hear about him when Baldr dies and Odin sends him to Hel to inquire about getting Baldr back. See Baldr in chapters.

Hildr: person, Valkyrie. One of the Valkyries. See Valkyries in chapters.

Himinbjörg: place, the castle or home of Heimdallur. See Heimdallur in chapters.

Hjörþrimul: person, Valkyrie. One of the Valkyries. See Valkyries in chapters.

Hliðskjálf: place, high seat. The high seat that Odin sits on when he is in Valhalla.

Hnitbjorg: place, mountain. The mountain where Gunnlöð was exiled to protect the mead of poetry. Odin burrowed through the mountain to steal the mead. See Odin in chapters.

Hoddmímir's Wood: place. Possibly Yggdrasil, but either way, the wood where Lífþrasir and Líf emerge after Ragnarök to reintroduce humanity to the world.

Hoenir: person, god. A travel companion of Odin. Little is known of him except that he is purported to have been part of the trio to create Ask and Embla (Ash and Elm) at the beginning of time. Also indirectly responsible for the beheading of Mimir.

Hotherus: person, human. Possible alternate persona for Höðr. See Baldr in chapters.

Höðr: person, god. Blind son of Odin and brother of Baldr. See Höðr in chapters.

Hrungnir: person, giant. Owner of Gullfaxi. He bet Odin his horse was faster, and later, after angering Odin and fighting Thor, he lost his head in a fight with the god of thunder. See Thor in chapters.

Hvergelmir: place, well. One of the three water sources that hydrates Yggdrasil. This well is in Niflheim.

Hymir: person, giant. Father of Týr. See Týr in chapters.

Idavoll: place. The plains of Asgard where the gods often meet to discuss matters of urgency. This will be the meeting place of the new gods after Ragnarök.

Iðunn: person, goddess. Wife of Bragi and keeper of the magic fruit that grants immortality to the gods. See Iðunn in chapters.

innangarðr: idea. A more civilized home place. One of order and discipline. Less wild than útangarðr.

Járngreipr: thing, gloves. The iron gloves of Thor, used when handling Mjölnir. See Thor in chapters.

Járnsaxa: person, giant. With Thor, mother of Magni and Móði.

Jörd: person, giant. Mother of Thor. See Thor in chapters.

Jörmungandr: animal, Midgard Serpent. Son of Loki and Angrboða. Will kill Thor at Ragnarök. See Ragnarök in chapters.

Kaupang: place, a medieval Norse term for trading city, but eventually used to denote a specific trading village on the east coast of Viksfjord, Norway.

Kvasir: person, human. Created from the spittle of all the Æsir and Vanir to be the wisest human. Killed by Fjalar and Galar. See Odin in chapters.

Kvasir: thing, mead. Created from the human Kvasir. Recovered by Odin. See Odin in chapters.

Líf: person, human. The only male to survive Ragnarök by hiding in Hoddmímir's Wood. He will repopulate the world with his lover, Lífþrasir.

Lífþrasir: person, human. The only female to survive Ragnarök by hiding in Hoddmímir's Wood. She will repopulate the world with her lover, Líf.

Lokasenna: thing, poem of the *Poetic Edda* about Loki's capture and confinement. See Loki in chapters.

Loki: person, giant. Trickster of Asgard. With Angrboða, father of Hel, Fenrir, and Jörmungandr. With Svaðilfari, mother of Sleipnir. With Sigyn father of Nari (Narfi) and Vali. Will help usher in Ragnarök. See Loki in chapters.

Magni: person, god. Son of Thor and Járnsaxa.

Mani: person, human. The son of Mundilfari, forced to drive the chariot of the moon until Ragnarök.

Megingjörd: thing, belt. Thor's belt that, when he dons it, doubles his strength in battle. See Thor in chapters.

Merseburg Incantations: thing, spells. The only two known pagan spells from the tenth century in German. Written in Old High German, they were discovered in a Christian book of the ninth century. They are kept in the church chapel of Merseburg.

Midgard: place, realm. The world where humans live. Connected to Asgard by Bifröst the rainbow bridge; it is the centermost world of the cosmos.

Miðgarðr: thing. The great wall that encircles Midgard. It was created from the eyelashes of the giant Ymir and is meant to protect humans from the other beings of the eight realms.

Mimir's Well: place, well. See Mimisbrunnr.

Mimisbrunnr: place, well. A more traditional name for Mimir's Well found in Jotunheim. It is here that Odin sacrificed an eye for knowledge.

Mistletoe: thing, plant. The only item, living or dead, that did not agree to not harm Baldr. See mistletoe in chapters.

Mjölnir: thing, hammer. The hammer of Thor. See Mjölnir in chapters.

Móði: person, god. Son of Thor and Járnsaxa.

Móðguðr: person, giantess. The giant maiden who guards the bridge Gjallarbú. See Hel in chapters.

Mundilfari: person, human. The father of Sol and Mani.

Muspelheim: place, realm. The land of fire. Home to Surtr who, with his fire, began the process of creation. See Surtr in chapters.

Naglfar: thing, boat. A boat made from the nails of all the dead in Helheim. At Ragnarök, Naglfar will break its moorings and ferry the giants to Ragnarök.

Nanna: person, goddess. Wife of Baldr. Nanna dies of a broken heart after her husband is killed, and she is burned on his funeral pyre to be with him in Helheim. See Nanna in chapters.

Narfi: person, giant. Also known as Nari. See below.

Nari: person, giant. Son of Loki. Also referred to as Narfi. Killed by Odin to use his intestines to bind the trickster to the stone after being captured by Thor. See Loki in chapters.

Náströnd: place, Helheim. Hall of corpses made up of the direst of those who died after Ragnarök. The serpent Niðhöggr feasts on the corpses. See Hel in chapters.

Nat: person, giant. Mother of Dag. Put in the sky to drive the chariot of night.

Nerthus: person, Vanir. Possible twin sister of Njörðr and possible mother to Freyja and Freyjr. See Njörðr in chapters.

Nidavellir: place, realm. Another name for Svartalfheim.

Niflheim: place, realm. The realm of ice and cold. Often accredited as being where Helheim is located, but just as often Helheim is its own realm. Instrumental in the creation of all things.

Niðhöggr: animal, serpent. The great serpent that gnaws at the base of Yggdrasil before Ragnarök. Ratatoskr relays insults between the great serpent and the eagle with no name at the top of the tree. See Hel in chapters.

Njörðr: person, Vanir. Father of Freyjr and Freyja. See Njörðr in chapters.

Nordi: person, dwarf. The dwarf that holds up the northern corner of the skull of Ymir, creating the sky.

Norður: direction. Icelandic for *north.*

Norns: persons, giantesses. The three women who weave our fates when we are born. Urðr represents the past in all of us, Verðandi is our present situation, and Skuld is what is to come. They live near Urðarbrunnr in a hall at the base of the great ash tree Yggdrasil. That which the Norns dictate must come to pass.

Odin: person, god. All Father and leader of all the gods. See Odin in chapters.

Ogham: thing, alphabet. The stick language writing used by the Irish people between the fourth and tenth centuries CE. The writing is a series of straight lines crossed at points to differentiate the letters in the alphabet.

Öðr: person, god. The husband of Freyja, who often left his wife to go on journeys.

Ótr: person, dwarf. A dwarf with the ability to change into an otter. While in that form one day, he was killed by Loki when Loki, Odin, and Hœnir were out travelling. When they arrived at the home of Hreidmar they showed the old man the pouch that Loki made from the skin of the otter. Hreidmar recognized his son immediately and took the gods by force, telling Loki that he would kill the others if Loki did not fill the otter pouch with gold. Loki did that and brought it back but the gold that he used was cursed.

Ragnarök: occurrence. The end of the worlds and the beginning of the next. See Ragnarök in chapters.

Ratatoskr: animal, squirrel. A squirrel that carries insults up and down Yggdrasil between Niðhöggr at the roots and an unnamed eagle at the crown of the tree.

Regin: person, dwarf. Son of Hreidmar and brother to Fafnir. He convinces his foster son Sigurd to kill Fafnir but plots to kill Sigurd for all the gold after Fafnir is dead.

Rindr: person, giant. Impregnated by Odin to birth Váli and seek revenge upon Höðr for the death of Baldr. See Baldr in chapters.

Saxo Grammaticus: person, human. Author of the *Gesta Danorum*, which is the first full history of Denmark.

Seiðr: thing, magic. Magic usually practiced by women but also practiced by Odin after hanging from Yggdrasil.

Sigurd: person, human. The foster son of Regin and foster nephew of Fafnir. Sigurd is convinced by Regin to kill Fafnir for the gold he protects.

Sigyn: person, giantess. The wife of Loki, Sigyn sits next to her husband until Ragnarök, holding a bowl above his head to keep the venom from the serpent from harming him. See Loki in chapters.

Sinmara: person, giantess. Possibly the wife of Surtr. See Surtr in chapters.

Skadi: person, giantess. Daughter of Þjazi. Wife of Njörðr. See Njörðr in chapters.

Skirnir: person, god. Servant of Freyjr. Sent to Jotunheim to woo the giantess Gerðr for Freyjr. See Freyjr in chapters.

Skirnismál: thing, poem, the poem of Freyjr wooing the giantess Gerðr. See Freyjr in chapters.

Skíðblaðnir: thing, boat. The finest of all boats. This boat belongs to Freyjr and is able to be "folded" and placed in a pocket when not needed.

Skoll: wolf, giant. One of two wolves to chase Sol and Mani around the world until they consume them at Ragnarök.

Skögul: person, Valkyrie. One of the Valkyries. See Valkyries in chapters.

Skuld: person, Norn. The goddess of the future. One of the three Norns.

Sleipnir: animal, horse. Sleipnir is the eight-legged horse ridden by Odin. The horse was the product of Loki in mare form and the giant's horse Svaðilfari. See Sleipnir in chapters.

Sol: person, human. The daughter of Mundilfari, forced to drive the chariot of the sun until Ragnarök.

Sons of Ivaldi: persons, dwarves. The dwarves that made the golden hair of Sif.

Sturluson, Snorri: person, human. Snorri was an Icelander, poet, writer, and member of the Icelandic Althing. He is the author of the *Prose* or *Younger Edda.*

Sudri: person, dwarf. The dwarf that holds up the southern corner of the skull of Ymir, creating the sky.

Surtr: person, giant. Surtr will ultimately be responsible for burning all of creation at Ragnarök. See Surtr in chapters.

Suttung: person, giant. Son of Gilling. Captured Galar and Fjalar and ransomed their lives for the mead of poetry, brewed from the blood of Kvasir. See Odin in chapters.

Suður: direction. Icelandic for *south.*

Svartalfheim: place, realm. Home of the dark elves, also referred to as dwarves. It is a world of darkness and endless tunnels and smithies.

Svaðilfari: animal, horse. Sire to Sleipnir, with Loki as mare. See Sleipnir in chapters.

Thor: person, god. Son of Odin and Jord. See Thor in chapters.

Thrym: person, giant. King of the Jotnar. Thrym lives at his palace in Útgarðr.

Týr: person, giant. Týr is the god responsible for binding Fenrir by tricking him into wearing Gleipnir. He sacrificed his hand for this. See Týr in chapters.

Ullr: person, god. Son of Sif. God of archery and the hunt. See Ullr in chapters.

Urvandill: person, god. Possibly the father of Ullr, with the goddess Sif. See Sif in chapters.

Urðr: person, Norn. The goddess who sees the past.

Urðr's Well: place, Asgard. The well of the Norns. Here the Norns water the great tree Yggdrasil.

Urðarbrunnr: place, Asgard. The hall of the Norns at the base of Yggdrasil at the mouth of Urðr's Well.

Útgarðr: place, Jotunheim. The capital city of the Jotnar.

Útgarða-Loki: person, giant. The chief of the castle of Útgarða in Jotunheim. See Jörmungandr in chapters.

útangarðr: idea. A place of danger and unpredictability. Less civilized than innangarðr.

Valhalla: place, great hall. Valhalla is Odin's great hall of fallen warriors. The hall has a roof of shields in golden bright, rafters of spears, and seats of breastplates. In the *Grimnismál* it states that there are five hundred and forty doors that eight hundred warriors may exit at the same time. The hall is home to the einherjar, the fallen warriors that fight and feast until they are needed at Ragnarök.

Vali: person, giant. See Nari.

Váli: person, god. Son of Odin and Rindr. Conceived specifically to kill Höðr after the death of Baldr. See Baldr in chapters.

Valknut: thing, symbol. An interwoven triple triangle that might represent a number of things. See Valknut in chapters.

Valkyrie: person, goddess. Women warriors who choose who may live and who may die in battle. Those who are chosen to die are taken to either Valhalla or Folkvang. See Valkyries in chapters.

Vanaheim: place, realm. Home of the Vanir. In the *Poetic Edda*, Vanaheim is said to be west of Asgard, but that is relative since the great tree Yggdrasil is vast, and in a three-dimensional relationship worlds may be found differently and who is to say what is west.

Vanir: race, god or goddess. Those who live in Vanaheim. Freyjr, Freyja, and Njörðr are Vanir.

Ve: person, god. Son of Bor and Bestla. Brother to Vili and Odin.

Verðandi: person, Norn. The goddess of the present. One of the three Norns.

Vestri: person, dwarf. The dwarf who holds up the western corner of the skull of Ymir, creating the sky.

Vestur: direction. Icelandic for *west*.

Veðrfölnir: animal, hawk. The hawk that sits between the eyes of the great unnamed eagle at the top of Yggdrasil.

Viðar: person, god. Son of Odin who kills Fenrir.

Vili: person, god. Son of Bor and Bestla. Brother to Ve and Odin.

Völva: person, god or human. A woman capable of seeing the future. Those considered völvas are usually seen with a metal wand and graves with bent wands have been uncovered.

Völuspá: thing, poem. Part of the *Poetic Edda*, it tells of the beginning and ending of the world.

Yggdrasil: thing, tree. The great ash tree that connects all nine realms to each other. See Yggdrasil in chapters.

Ymir: person, giant. Ymir is the first living creature formed from the contact of fire and ice. He is a giant who can create life without another. As he slept in the great cosmos of space, other giants were born from the sweat of his armpits and between his legs.

Ynglinga: thing, saga. One of Snorri's sagas that tells of the exploits of Odin.

Þjazi: person, giant. In an eagle disguise, Þjazi forced Loki into promising him the fruit of Iðunn or be dropped to his death. Killed by the Asgardians after kidnapping Iðunn. See Iðunn in chapters.

Þrymheimr: place, castle. Home to Þjazi in Jotunheim.

Þőkk: person, giantess. A giant witch who refuses to mourn for Baldr, allowing Hel to keep the fallen god in Helheim. Thought to be Loki in disguise. See Loki in chapters.

Þrúðr: person, god. Daughter of Thor and Sif. See Thor in chapters.

Æsir: people, gods, indigenous population of Asgard.

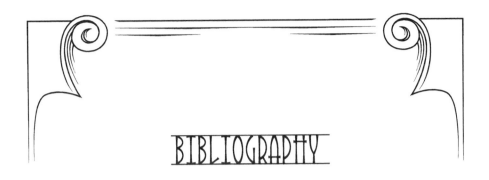

BIBLIOGRAPHY

Byock, Jesse, trans. *The Prose Edda: Norse Mythology.* By Snorri Sturluson. London: Penguin, 2005.

Davidson, H. R. Ellis. *Gods and Myths of the Viking Age.* London: Penguin Press, 1964.

Einarsson, Stefân. *Icelandic: Grammar, Text, Glossary.* London: Johns Hopkins University Press, 1994.

Faulkes, Anthony, ed. *Two Versions of Snorra Edda from the 17th Century. 2 vols.* Reykjavik: Stofnun Árna Magnússonar, 1979.

Girotti, Ken, dir. *Vikings.* Season 3, episode 1, "Mercenary." Written by Michael Hirst, featuring Travis Fimmel, Katheryn Winnick, Clive Standen. Aired February 19, 2015, on the History Channel.

Grundy, Stephan. "Freyja and Frigg." In *The Concept of the Goddess,* edited by Sandra Billington and Miranda Green, 55–57. London: Routledge, 1998.

Hastrup, Kirsten. *Culture and History in Medieval Iceland: An Anthropological Analysis of Structure and Change.* Oxford: Oxford University Press, 1985.

Ingstad, Helge. "Vinland Ruins Prove Vikings Found the New World." *National Geographic.* National Geographic Society. Washington, DC. 126, no. 5 (November 1964): 708–734.

Larrington, Carolyne, trans. *The Poetic Edda*. Oxford World's Classics. London: Oxford Press, 1996.

Lindow, John. *Norse Mythology: A Guide to the Gods, Heroes, Rituals, and Beliefs*. New York: Oxford University Press, 2001.

"Midgard." Online Etymology Dictionary. Douglas Harper. Accessed May 24, 2020. https://www.etymonline.com/word/Midgard.

Njarðvík, Teresa Dröfn Freysdóttir, ed. *Runes: The Icelandic Book of Fuþark*. Translated by Philip Roughton. Reykjavik: Icelandic Magic Company, 2018.

Page, R. I. *Norse Myths*. Austin: University of Texas Press, 2001.

Seigfried, Karl E. H., ed. *The Illustrated Völuspá: The Prophecy of the Seeress*. Nashville: Fateful Signs, 2018.

Taylor, Catherine. *Norse Myths & Tales: Anthology of Classic Tales*. Fulham, United Kingdom: Flame Tree Publishing, 2018.

Teague, Gypsey. *Fangs and Claws*. Scott's Valley, CA: CreateSpace, 2012.

———. *Three Years of Winter: Ragnarok Is No Longer a Myth*. Scott's Valley, CA: CreateSpace.

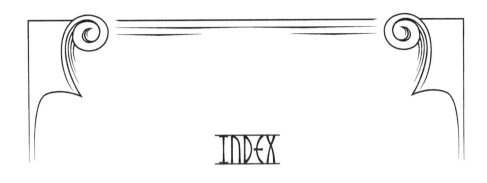

INDEX

G

H

To Write to the Author

If you wish to contact the author or would like more information about this book, please write to the author in care of Llewellyn Worldwide Ltd. and we will forward your request. Both the author and publisher appreciate hearing from you and learning of your enjoyment of this book and how it has helped you. Llewellyn Worldwide Ltd. cannot guarantee that every letter written to the author can be answered, but all will be forwarded. Please write to:

Gypsey Elaine Teague
℅ Llewellyn Worldwide
2143 Wooddale Drive
Woodbury, MN 55125-2989

Please enclose a self-addressed stamped envelope for reply,
or $1.00 to cover costs. If outside the U.S.A., enclose
an international postal reply coupon.

Many of Llewellyn's authors have websites with additional information and resources. For more information, please visit our website at http://www.llewellyn.com